What People Are Saying About

Breathing with Missoku

A peach tree of surprise.
Morihide Katayama, Record Geijutsu

It is astonishing to learn that everything can be changed by mastering Missoku.
Seiko Ito, Senken-Nikki

Breathing like a dream.
Yumi Yamagata, NHK-BS2 Weekly Book Review

Breathing with Missoku

The Undiscovered Zen Secret of
Japanese Culture

Breathing with Missoku

The Undiscovered Zen Secret of Japanese Culture

Akikazu Nakamura

Translated by Robin Thompson

BOOKS

London, UK
Washington, DC, USA

CollectiveInk

First published by O-Books, 2024
O-Books is an imprint of Collective Ink Ltd.,
Unit 11, Shepperton House, 89 Shepperton Road, London, N1 3DF
office@collectiveinkbooks.com
www.collectiveinkbooks.com
www.o-books.com

For distributor details and how to order please visit the 'Ordering' section on our website.

Text copyright: Akikazu Nakamura, 2023

ISBN: 978 1 80341 700 4
978 1 80341 724 0 (ebook)
Library of Congress Control Number: 2023949995

A CIP catalogue record for this book is available from the British Library.

Design: Lapiz Digital Services

UK: Printed and bound by CPI Group (UK) Ltd, Croydon, CR0 4YY
Printed in North America by CPI GPS partners

The authors of this book do not dispense medical advice or prescribe the use of any technique as a form of treatment for physical, emotional, or medical problems without the advice of a physician, either directly or indirectly. The intent of the authors is only to offer information of a general nature to help you in your quest for emotional and spiritual well-being. In the event you use any of the information in this book for yourself, which is your constitutional right, the authors and the publisher assume no responsibility for your actions.

We operate a distinctive and ethical publishing philosophy in all areas of our business, from our global network of authors to production and worldwide distribution.

Why Does That Person's Voice Come Through?
Written in Japanese
ISBN: 978-4-344-97651-1

Japanese Breathing Technique
Written in Japanese
ISBN: 978-4-8142-0536-3

'Missoku' Changes the Body
Written in Japanese
ISBN: 978-4-10-603563-4

Overtones: A Cultural Journal of Sound,
Language, and the Body
Written in Japanese
ISBN: 978-4-3939-5704-2

Contents

Preface

This publication of *Breathing with Missoku* has been over 20 years in the making. First published in Japan to reawaken a dormant tradition amongst the Japanese people, I now invite the rest of the world to join us. Missoku is the genesis of Japanese culture and it can be found flickering in the shadows of all Japanese traditions — an everlasting flame. However, its benefits are not exclusive to Japan; in fact, it can be applied to various activities including, but not limited to, martial arts, music and sports. I hope you enjoy the discovery of Missoku as much as I did.

Acknowledgements

I would like to express my sincere gratitude to Masako Azetsu for being the backbone behind this book for its first publication in 2006. Secondly, I'd like to thank Julia Hill for making the Collective Ink publication possible. I would not have been able to publish this edition without your application writing and manuscript editing skills! Further thanks go to Ray Brooks for showing us the way to publishing overseas. I appreciate your help and our long friendship. Finally, thank you to my wife, Masako Nakamura, and my son, Satoshi Nakamura, for your never-ending love and support.

Part I

Discovery of Missoku

Introduction

Missoku Is the Key

Missoku, or *esoteric breathing*, is the technique I use when performing. It's completely different from the technique of breathing from the abdomen and from the chest employed in Western music.

Missoku is a method of breathing that I encountered as I worked on my *shakuhachi* performance technique. I came to realise that this isn't a breathing technique unique to shakuhachi performers and that it's essentially a method of breathing that's been employed quite naturally in Japan since ancient times. For those who are new to the shakuhachi, it is a traditional Japanese bamboo flute with five holes. It was used in Zen Buddhism practices.

To describe Missoku in simple terms, you lower your centre of gravity by pressing down and outwards on the pelvis and maintain a pose with the abdomen extended slightly when both inhaling and exhaling. You then take deep breaths without tensing or moving the body in a manner that involves raising and lowering the diaphragm, employing internal rather than external muscles. This method of breathing makes it possible to inhale and exhale very large quantities of air in a single breath, with the body itself remaining stable and calm. It brings about an increase in powers of concentration on a mental level whilst at the same time engendering a sense of freedom and liberation.

People today lead a wide variety of lifestyles and rash generalisations need to be avoided, but there are certain impressions we gain as we look around at what is happening in society. The societies of most advanced countries seem to be growing more and more enervated by the day, with people experiencing anxiety, claustrophobia, lack of communication, impatience and lethargy. Many people are unwilling to face up to the basics of everyday life and reject the idea of working to support themselves or of getting married and raising children. Indeed, such people often have no interest even in pursuing happiness in their own lives, with their inability to place trust in themselves, in the society to which they belong, and in their own inner strength. In Japan in particular, there are those who are unaware of the richness and splendour of their nation's traditional culture and who take no pride in it. Having passed through the rough seas of the Second World War and the subsequent long years of economic regeneration, Japan now enjoys a degree of prosperity it has never known before. Why then has our society become so fatigued?

It seems to me that this enervation is a warning sign issuing from the body. Although we face no obvious threats such as war and starvation, the sense of existential crisis that many of us feel deep within us gives rise to anxiety and a tendency to be either overly self-protective or overly aggressive. What is happening to us physically?

Japanese people tend to get nervous in situations where Westerners might be more inclined to get tense and use this tension as a stimulus to concentration. It's often noted that Japanese athletes, for example, fail to demonstrate their potential to the full at the Olympics and in international competitions. Similarly, many Japanese people will have had the experience of finding their voices becoming pinched and their breathing quickened when called upon to speak or sing in public. The reasons for this include inability to communicate and lack of autogenic training. But it's interesting to compare Japanese people today with their compatriots in the late nineteenth century. At the start of the Meiji era, former *samurai* travelled to Europe and America with no prior knowledge of European languages. Wherever they went they were praised for their composure and dignity. Japanese athletes shortly before and after the Second World War were sent to the Berlin and Melbourne Olympics, where they put up a fine showing against Western athletes with far superior physiques. What was it that enabled them to be so successful?

In the past, Japanese people sat on the floor on *tatami* mats, wore *kimono* with *obi* sashes tied tightly around their waist, and engaged in physical work in the fields or as practitioners of a specific craft. With their feet placed firmly on the ground and their stable posture with the pelvis lowered, they naturally practised Missoku breathing. A hundred years after the start of the Meiji era, they were sitting in chairs facing a table, wearing Western style clothing and moving around in vehicles rather than on their feet.

This change in lifestyle has resulted in Japanese people losing the strength that they formerly possessed in the lower half of the body and many of the skills involved in using their bodies. On the other hand, they still haven't really mastered the Western technique of breathing from the abdomen, which requires strong superficial abdominal muscles in order to ventilate while maintaining a posture with the pelvis upright.

Although nutritional improvements have resulted in the Japanese physique coming closer to that of ethnic Europeans, ethnic Japanese aren't equipped with the same bone structure and muscles, meaning that they necessarily breathe from the chest rather than the abdomen. Japanese people today tend, therefore, to take shallow, fast breaths, just as we all do when we're feeling anxious, facing a crisis or feeling nervous.

Considerable research has been done in recent years on traditional Japanese physical culture. Researchers such as Takashi Saitō and Yoshinori Kōno have thrown fresh light from a new perspective on the importance of the physical sensation of lowering the centre of gravity onto the pelvis and abdomen. Their analyses are particularly impressive and convincing. But with our increasing reliance on our minds rather than our bodies and the dramatic decrease in the use of our bodies as a whole that are among the features of modern life, I wonder how we can put their recommendations into practice. I feel that the key to this lies with breathing.

Every person breathes. Life itself is essentially an activity made possible through the ongoing accumulation of breaths. Try deep breathing. You'll find that your body relaxes and that tension in your head decreases. But it isn't possible to keep this up for long. If you deliberately try to breathe deeper than usual, you'll soon get tired through the effort, and it's difficult to keep it up anyway whilst you're doing other things. On the other hand, if you continue breathing slowly and gently without thinking about it too much, your body will naturally adopt a particular posture. This isn't a posture assumed as a result of conscious thought but rather one that the body naturally assumes.

This is a demonstration of the *culture of breath* that lies dormant within the body at work. Although Japanese people may be gradually losing the traditional skills that previously played important roles in our daily lives and in society, their bodies are still able to recall them through ancestral memory. It should be clear to everyone that continuing to breathe in this manner ushers in a sense of mental relaxation and more acute sensory perception. Out of necessity and in connection with my occupation as a performer, I looked into methods of stable, deep breathing. The process of trial and error in this regard occupied me for a long time. It all seems so simple once you get the hang of it, but it's this method of breathing that may be thought of as the traditional Japanese method.

I found that the practice of Missoku resulted in a heightening of the senses and in a complete transformation of the world around me. I rediscovered too that this forms part of the same undercurrent that underpins the hidden richness of Japanese culture. I'd like here to describe my own pilgrimage through the world of Missoku and to consider the connection between Missoku and Japanese culture.

In the past, Japanese people acquired a method of deep, slow and relaxed breathing. I hope that you too will make the effort to regain this rich and ancient *culture of breath*.

Chapter 1

A Breath Pilgrimage

'Try blowing like this!' was the instruction given to me by the elderly master after he'd placed a bamboo leaf picked from the garden on the table. My instructor on this occasion was a hale and hearty monk in his late 70s belonging to a *Komusō* temple in Hakata.

It was in the autumn of 2000. For several years prior to this I'd been working on collecting the classical repertory of the Komusō shakuhachi with the aim of bringing this tradition back to life once again. I travelled to visit transmitters of the Komusō shakuhachi tradition at Komusō temples throughout Japan. I learned pieces handed down the ages in different regions and recorded them for release on CD in an effort to present this music to modern audiences. I started off in the Tsugaru region, after which I decided to go down to Kyushu.

There are several schools or lineages of Komusō shakuhachi. My teacher's teacher was Watazumidōso, who hailed from Hakata. My intention in visiting Hakata was not just to come into contact with one of the foremost examples of the Komusō shakuhachi tradition, but also to search for my own roots as a performer of the shakuhachi.

In the past, Komusō monks would lead an itinerant existence as part of their spiritual training, and there has been a tradition of their temples opening their doors to visitors from far away. In line with this tradition, my own instructor on this occasion offered me a generous welcome. In a small tatami-matted room by the side of the main temple, I talked with him freely about the Komusō shakuhachi of Tsugaru, where I had been a recent visitor, and about the classical repertory. I showed him the musical notation of the Tsugaru pieces. I asked him to teach me the piece I showed him in the version that he knew, and he asked me first to play it to him. The piece in question was *Chōshi*, the most basic item in the Komusō repertory. I suppose I must have revealed a touch of bewilderment when he asked this of me.

I'd always thought that a good breathing technique was the most important aspect of shakuhachi performance and I'd studied it from many different perspectives. From the basics to applied techniques, I'd learned much from my shakuhachi teacher and from performers with far greater experience than me. I'd studied abdominal breathing techniques with singing teachers, chest breathing with a soprano singer, and applications of these techniques to wind instruments with performers of these instruments. I'd also mastered the technique of circular breathing.

I would spend an hour a day working on my own breathing technique. Perhaps because of this, things generally went well without my having to think too much about my technique, but I had little idea of the mechanism involved in what I was doing. Now I realise that I'd unconsciously acquired an outstanding breathing technique into which I would finally be able to gain some insight.

What slightly concerned me was that Watazumidōso had his own distinctive breathing technique that was referred to as Missoku. But there was nothing I could find about this technique in writing, and nobody seemed to be able to say anything definite about it. What this meant was that I'd got most of the way to achieving my goal in this respect, but there were still areas where I felt lacking in confidence. In contrast to the easygoing atmosphere that had prevailed in our conversation up to that point, my tension had clearly become palpable.

The master opened up the sliding doors and showed me a bamboo leaf that he'd picked up in the garden. 'Blow like this!'

he said. It was shortly before noon on a fine, late autumn day with bright blue skies above. I found it impossible to retain my composure, thinking of the piece I was about to play and of what the master had meant by the bamboo leaf, which seemed like a Zen riddle. Various thoughts were swirling around in my mind as I tried to concentrate with no distractions. I felt that I'd learn nothing in my present state of mind and would be unable to fulfil my objective. These thoughts weighed heavily on me.

My performance was nothing like as good as usual. My body was racked by tension and my breath intake was poor. Being inside an ancient temple also meant that the sound failed to project and got sucked in by the walls. In a performance environment with a good acoustic, the sound reverberates and it's easy to breathe. But in a traditional Japanese style room with little echo, the sound immediately cuts off, meaning that the player has little time to breathe before moving on to the next sound. Poor breathing inevitably results in inadequate intake of oxygen and makes it painful to play at all. This made me all the more tense. This chain reaction meant that my performance on this occasion was particularly disappointing. Once I'd finished playing and after a short pause, the master turned to me and pointed out that my breathing didn't appear to be going well. He suggested that he give me some instruction in breathing.

This suggestion put me in a quandary for a moment. I wondered if I shouldn't reply that I'd study it by myself. But at the same time, I had a feeling that I might learn something of unfathomable importance. With the Japanese proverb 'To ask may bring momentary shame, but not to ask and remain ignorant brings everlasting shame' in mind, I humbly asked him for his instruction.

In the small room in which I'd played the shakuhachi, we sat facing each other and he showed me his method of breathing. I pointed out that this was the same method as used by Watazumidōso. I'd at last encountered an explanation of how the Missoku breathing technique employed by Watazumidōso is done.

You begin by rounding your hips and lowering the pelvis and tilting it backwards and with the abdomen rounded and tilting forwards. You then maintain this abdominal posture as you breathe in through the nose and then exhale.

A degree of exertion is required to maintain this posture when you breathe, but my instructor did so with no effort whatsoever. In response to his question about whether I had ever practised *zazen* meditation, I replied that I had done so frequently on my visits to temples in various locations. He said that, in that case, I ought to be aware of how to breathe in this way, but clearly am not aware of how to do so. He then led me into the main temple so that we could practise zazen together.

We sat cross-legged in the zazen manner, and I tilted my pelvis downward, making sure that my upper body remained bolt upright.

'This is how we breathe when practising Zen meditation. You breathe in effortlessly and without thinking too much about inhaling and exhaling, gradually find that your breath is entering and leaving your body quite naturally. That's the feeling you need to cultivate,' he told me.

Everything now seemed to be ready. Realising that I was having problems with it, I'd been practising breathing every day and had used my own method to develop the technique of circular breathing. Because of the partial similarity with circular breathing, I found this method of breathing relatively easy to get the hang of.

That's it! Breathe in instantaneously. A large amount of air begins to flow inside the body. A sound drawn out as evenly as a line drawn with a ruler extends to infinity without the body moving in even the slightest degree. Is this what Missoku is all about?

Various thoughts spun around inside my head. As I slowly exhaled and inhaled, I recalled the bamboo leaf to which my instructor had referred to earlier. I recalled the graceful form of the young leaf with its vivid green colouration and felt that what my instructor was trying to tell me was that, when playing a piece, one should aim to convey a totally different atmosphere rather than limit oneself to narrow considerations such as producing a good, strong sound. Once the zazen session was over, we left the main temple for one of the smaller guest rooms and recommenced our discussion.

'Your problem is that you're suppressing your sound in an effort to produce a good quality tone. That's not the way to do it. You should blow as if in a state of emptiness.' My instructor addressed me in a gentle manner as the sun began to set. He then opened the sliding doors facing out onto the garden and said, 'This is emptiness!'

In front of me I saw a wide open space of a type that I'd never seen in Tokyo. As the sun set, the space as a whole was sinking into a shade of dark grey amidst which I could see the odd crimson persimmon.

I have yet to see that colour again, but whenever I perform, I think of this concept of emptiness. Performers tend to dissect the music we hear and to immerse ourselves in analytical considerations, noticing acutely when a rhythm is inaccurate or when a pitch is out of tune. But this method of breathing evokes a totally different dimension, as if the universe were something thrown wholesale before our very eyes.

This was my encounter with Missoku.

Attracted by Music

I'd always been fond of music. When I was five or six years old, I used to keep company with a girl living in my neighbourhood in order to listen in on her piano lessons. Although still a child,

I was aware I was making a nuisance of myself and so decided to ask my father if I could take piano lessons too. He replied that, as a boy, I'd be better off playing outdoors, which would benefit me physically and mentally far more than playing the piano. This made me all the more determined to learn a musical instrument. After reaching primary school age, I was happy to find that the harmonica and the recorder were part of the school music curriculum, and I learned a large number of pieces. After entering junior high school, my elder brother bought me a guitar, and I became immersed in the music of Peter, Paul and Mary, Bob Dylan, and Japanese folk. In my third year of junior high school, I became preoccupied with the electric guitar and especially with Jimi Hendrix. This was a passionate era when everyone entertained doubts about music, life and the status quo.

What nagged at me at the time was the question of why people thought that the distorted tone of the electric guitar was so great. Various techniques of considerable complexity were used to distort the sound of the instrument and I began to wonder why I and so many other people were so obsessed by such sonic distortion. I was also particularly attracted at this time by the *Tsugaru-shamisen* of Takahashi Chikuzan who, in the same manner as the electric guitar, employed a distorted, muddy tone on his instrument. One day I had the revelatory experience of listening to Tōru Takemitsu's *November Steps*. This was music that totally upturned my musical sensibility as a young man who, until then, had been obsessed solely with rock. This work featuring shakuhachi and *biwa* in solo roles was performed by an orchestra conducted by Seiji Ozawa. The sound of the shakuhachi was even more distorted than that of Jimi Hendrix's guitar. The instrument's tone was complex, free and broad in range to an extent that it's impossible to put into words. I made up my mind to learn this amazing instrument and telephoned a performer whose name I'd found in the telephone directory.

This marked my encounter with the great Katsuya Yokoyama, from whom I continued to learn for the rest of his life.

He asked me if I'd ever learned the shakuhachi previously and I replied that I was a complete beginner. He said with a chuckle that he'd never come across someone like me before, but he asked me to come along and see him anyway, an offer which I was more than happy to take up.

What astonished me when I started attending his lessons was the incredible musicianship he displayed. From the very outset, lessons involved the oral transmission of basic pieces from the Komusō repertory. The difficult pieces in this repertory convey the impression of listening to the recitation of a Buddhist sutra, and it's hard initially to make head or tail of them. I recorded these pieces on an endless tape that I listened to from morning until night until they'd entered the very core of my being.

The musical notation for the shakuhachi employs a system of syllabic mnemonics linked to specific melodic progressions. This system came into use during the Edo Period, although there are differences in how it was applied in the eastern (Kantō) and western (Kansai) regions of Japan. For example, the syllables *ro-tsu-re-chi-ri* as used in the Kantō region are replaced in Kansai by the syllables *fo-ho-u-e-ya,* which correspond to the pitches *re-fa-so-la-do* in the solfège system. There is no indication of rhythm and meter in this system of notation since these are thought of as elements that need to be experienced on the physical level. This means that it's the length of the performer's breath that is the decisive factor in determining the overall balance. Perhaps because of the freedom that this music grants to the performer, the more profound and the more interesting the music becomes as one becomes more proficient in its realisation.

But breathing proved to be a hard obstacle to overcome. The shakuhachi is an instrument that requires an enormous amount of breath, meaning that, for the performer, breathing and the time required to breathe as the music progresses can

17

prove to be a major challenge. They certainly did so as far as I was concerned. Although I'd learned the technique of breathing from the abdomen from singers of Western music, I found that it took too long to breathe using this technique.

I studied how outstanding performers of the flute and other Western wind instruments breathe as they perform and asked them directly about this. But I never felt that they were breathing in what I considered to be the optimum fashion. When there was little time to take a breath, they would use chest breathing and when they had the leeway to do so, they would employ breathing from the abdomen. For example, even such an exceptional flutist as Jean-Pierre Rampal would, in the middle of a performance, remove his lips from the mouthpiece and link breaths with a clearly audible sound of breath intake.

For performers of the shakuhachi and indeed of all wind instruments, breathing through the mouth means temporarily losing one's embouchure and then reshaping it once again. The fact that even the most outstanding Western performers employ such an irrational method of breathing convinced me that there was still plenty of scope for further progress in breathing technique.

In contrast, watching Japanese performers of the shakuhachi, the Japanese transverse flute, *Noh* chanting (*utai*) and folksong made me realise that these performers, or at least those over a certain age, had no problem with breathing. They were able to perform with minimal breath intake and without moving to even the smallest extent. At the time, I thought this was extraordinary, but I had no idea what was going on.

From Research Chemist to Shakuhachi Performer

I was raised in an ordinary household in which interest in music was encouraged although the idea of becoming a professional musician was considered outlandish. I was on the science side of the fence at school, and I'd decided to get a job in the chemical research sector of a company. But the aims of research in academia are very different from those in a corporate environment. At the time there was no enthusiasm for research that entailed the extensive costs necessitated by considerations of safety and the environment. I enjoyed the work I was doing, but it seemed pointless to engage in research work that reaped no benefits for society. I didn't want to feel any regrets about the path on which my life had embarked and so I decided to do what I really wanted to do, which was to play the shakuhachi professionally.

My income took a major hit, but by a stroke of good fortune my performance activities throughout Japan came to the attention of a band called Tokyo Kid Brothers, who asked me to join them for performances in New York, Washington and throughout the United States. My contribution met with an ecstatic reception in the *New York Times* and in much of the American press, and Tom Hogan, producer of the musicals *Hair* and *Jesus Christ Superstar,* came up with the idea of incorporating the shakuhachi in a solo capacity into his shows. This reception gave me confidence in my own abilities and confirmed in me my belief that the shakuhachi is a wonderful musical instrument. At the same time, I felt that I wanted to be able to compose and improvise in the same manner as musicians during the Edo Period, although I was aware that I still lacked the theoretical and technical capacity to do so.

It seemed to me that learning Western music was important from two main perspectives. First, it makes it possible to develop one's abilities as a composer and improviser and, second, it permits a deeper insight into Japanese music. When seen from a Western perspective, Japanese music may seem to have various missing features such as structure and harmony. In terms of Western compositional methodology, one may wonder why there is no sound at a particular moment or why more isn't made of a climax. Conversely, applying a Japanese sensibility after having passed through Western music theory, one might think that a particular moment in a piece is one where an atmosphere of tranquillity should prevail or where various noises should be emphasised. For example, in the case of Western music, a climax tends to be created by increasing the volume of sound or the number of notes, whereas in the case of shakuhachi music, tranquillity may define the climax of a piece. But personally, I wasn't sufficiently well equipped to think about such matters in a theoretical and systematic manner at that stage.

I decided therefore that what I wanted to do was to learn as much as possible in as short a time as possible in the context of a course in advanced methodology at a music college, although not necessarily one in Japan. I set my sights on entering Berklee College of Music in Boston, which enjoys a high reputation for the education it provides in jazz theory and composition. Berklee is the only music college where it's possible to study Western classical composition and the theory and practice of jazz improvisation. Its alumni include many illustrious Japanese jazz musicians including Sadao Watanabe, Toshiko Akiyoshi and Makoto Ozone. At the age of 29, I was able to attend Berklee thanks to a scholarship from the college and a grant from the Rockefeller Foundation.

Berklee is a jazz college where students majoring in composition must also specialise in a particular instrument. My choice of instrument was the shakuhachi. The college authorities were completely taken aback. Most people there had never even heard of the shakuhachi and there was no class that provided tuition in non-Western instruments. They tried to persuade me to play the flute or the guitar, which I'd had some experience playing in the past. But there would be nothing innovatory about playing the flute at a jazz college. I felt that I wanted to stick to the shakuhachi, simply because of the almost insuperable challenge it presented. I stressed that I was determined to follow the course of study on this instrument.

A basic part of the course at Berklee consists of private lessons given by professors to individual students. At the start of their studies, the student is unable to choose the professor they want to study with, and the allocation of a particular teacher to a particular student is carried out by the college. The teacher to whom I was assigned was a saxophonist who was a master of bebop but showed almost no interest in any other type of music. When he saw my instrument, this exponent of an outdated genre of orthodox jazz seemed astonished and asked me whether my instrument wasn't some work of art. He began to play his sax and then asked me if I knew what he was playing. He said it was bebop. I replied that I couldn't do it yet, but that this was precisely what I'd come to America to study. He said that I'd never be able to do it and that I ought to go back to Japan. I said there's no way I'd be going back to Japan because I was absolutely determined to get to grips with this music.

Anyhow, the upshot was that I had to go and see the Chair of the Woodwind Department to get his permission to continue. His name was Joseph Viola, an eminent saxophonist who had taught Sadao Watanabe among many others. He said he'd seen the shakuhachi being played with the Boston Philharmonic and that he'd thought it was an instrument of enormous potential. But he pointed out that we were in America, implying that I should think about majoring on a different instrument. He suggested anyway that I should give him some idea of the possibilities of the shakuhachi by improvising on the instrument while he accompanied me on the piano. I began improvising in a jazz idiom, passing through a range of different keys. It all went well. After hearing me play, Professor Viola said that he reckoned I could be taught on the shakuhachi after all. The bebop professor reluctantly assented and told me to come along to his classroom where, on that very day, I had my first lesson.

He treated me like an adopted son and taught me considerately and conscientiously how to create the feel and the phrasing of

Black music. But what surprised me first of all was the absence of main beats when he accompanied me on the piano. I pointed out that I found it difficult to play with him because all the main beats were missing. He apologised but pointed out that this was how he felt the music. Having realised how important this question of *feeling* was, my sessions with him proved to be increasingly fruitful and enjoyable.

During the next academic year, I studied with a flutist who was strong on theory. In the case of pieces with extremely difficult modulations, he'd tell me to write down all the pitches I could play bar by bar and select those that were shared by the shakuhachi and by the piece in each modulated form. There are various common pitches even when one is faced by a series of modulations. Even when there were just one or two pitches playable in a particular key on the shakuhachi, my teacher suggested I should improvise around those pitches. This would demonstrate the positive qualities of my instrument and would show how the shakuhachi could avoid lapsing into musical tedium even when only one or two pitches were available.

Focusing on the instrument from a different angle, he thus enabled me to discover new possibilities for the shakuhachi. He had a thorough, logical understanding of music and his lessons gave me plenty of food for thought. On the occasion of my final lesson, just before I was due to graduate, I presented him with a special request. I asked him to teach me some special techniques that he'd held in reserve up until that point. He paused for thought and then said that he'd teach me some of the most advanced techniques currently available on the flute.

I was astonished to find that all the techniques that he imparted to me were standard on the shakuhachi. One of these was tone colour trills. Trills are normally performed on adjacent pitches, but tone colour trills involve rapid alternation between different tone colours on the same pitch. This is a technique known in shakuhachi terminology as *korokoro* or *karakara*.

22

'You mean like this,' I said and showed him how it was done on the shakuhachi. He was surprised to see how easily it could be done on my instrument and suggested we move on to the next technique, which involved sticking a piece of adhesive tape onto a part of the flute. He showed me how you can produce interesting noise-like effects using a wide embouchure.

'You mean like this,' I said again and gave him a display of noise effects on the shakuhachi. He was astonished to see how I could achieve the same effect without the use of adhesive tape.

The next technique he went on to explain involved closing all the keys and then slowly opening the holes above the keys to create a sound that rises slowly in pitch. This is a technique that can be realised almost effortlessly on the shakuhachi. My teacher then made the observation that it seemed that Western flutists had developed these techniques that he had been showing me in an attempt to catch up with the techniques traditionally employed by the shakuhachi.

This was my final lesson. I felt that I'd now come full circle. Having travelled the world, I was now able finally to return to my roots.

Performance at the International Contemporary
Music Festival in Berlin.

'Be the First': The Circular Breathing Method

Back in Japan in 1986, I set about using the shakuhachi as my means for creating new music. There was little precedent for such activity at the time. People would assume that composition by a shakuhachi performer meant writing music in either the classical shakuhachi idiom or in the genre of folksong. The idea of a shakuhachi performer writing music for string quartet or for a rock band was essentially unheard of. Nevertheless, my aim was to bring out and demonstrate the full range of the shakuhachi in such unconventional contexts.

There is currently an enormous number of players and fans of the shakuhachi in the West. Indeed, the instrument is in the process of taking root to the same extent as karate and Japanese cuisine. Many people are attracted by the vast tonal resources of this unusual instrument, ranging from the crystalline, sine wave-like purity of tone in its upper register to its distorted noise-like tone full of complex harmonics, although most people tend to be captivated initially by the manner in which the shakuhachi evokes a uniquely Oriental atmosphere. But despite this, the number of shakuhachi players in Japan, and especially players of the Komusō shakuhachi, is relentlessly decreasing. Only a minority of Japanese people these days are likely to have even heard the sound of a shakuhachi. I felt it was my task to demonstrate the attractions of the instrument.

In order to do this, I sensed that what was needed was to conduct a detailed analysis of the classical repertory from the standpoint of Western music theory and then, conversely, to analyse the music in order to reveal what was specifically Japanese about it. Having dismantled the music in this way, the task would be to reassemble it, to make it clearer to my contemporaries and, first and foremost, to convey what it is that makes the shakuhachi such an attractive instrument. What Glenn Gould had done with the keyboard music of J.S. Bach was in a sense what I wanted to do with the music of the Komusō shakuhachi.

I'd been taught more or less how to breathe from the abdomen by my shakuhachi teacher, and before going to Berklee I had essentially mastered the technique after receiving further instruction from Western-style singing teachers. This meant that I didn't feel in any sense inadequate in an American environment where abdominal breathing was generally practised by wind players, although I must admit that I did feel there was something subtly different between my method of playing and theirs. Abdominal breathing is tough on the shakuhachi, which is perhaps the world's least efficient wind instrument when it comes to the amount of breath required. Although I had no particular problems when I was playing jazz, when I played pieces from the classical Komusō repertory I felt that I was constantly having problems knowing where to breathe.

After returning from the United States, I therefore began working on the technique of circular breathing, which involves exhaling and inhaling at the same time, thus obviating the need to interrupt the flow of the music by taking breaths. There's a saxophonist named Ned Rosenberg who has a reputation as the greatest master of the circular breathing technique on his instrument. He's able to play for 20 – 30 minutes without a break while incorporating multiphonics. I heard that he also played the shakuhachi. I became friends with him after meeting him in New York. This led to me taking part in a concert with him in Japan in which I played a piece that he'd composed for the shakuhachi.

He told me that it was simple to circular breathe on the saxophone, but he found it impossible to do so on the shakuhachi. That gives some idea of how difficult it is to breathe on the instrument. While we were having this discussion, he turned to me and said of all of a sudden 'Aki, be the first!' He was encouraging me to be the first shakuhachi player to master the technique of circular breathing. His words set me on the path to achieving precisely that.

I practised the technique for hours every day. I soon got hold of the technique of storing air in my cheeks while inhaling through the nose, but it proved incredibly difficult to play the shakuhachi in this way. As I pointed out earlier, the shakuhachi requires enormous reserves of breath because of the instrument's wide bore. Moreover, there are no keys on the instrument, meaning that you have to use your embouchure to create tonal effects and inflections of pitch. Storing air inside the cheeks means that it's no longer possible to exert control over your embouchure.

But after days, months and indeed years of working on it, the eureka moment eventually arrived. I realised there was little effect on the embouchure if and when I was able to store the air not in my cheeks but at the back of my throat. I'd never heard of anyone doing this before, but I found that I didn't run out of breath when I managed to do it. It still took several more years before I felt confident enough to employ this technique in live performances. Indeed, it took a good ten years before I felt I'd really perfected the technique.

For a professional shakuhachi player, this represented an enormous leap from performing under the limitations imposed by the length of a single breath and the need to interrupt the musical flow by taking in new breaths all the time. During the mid-1990s, I found myself being extensively praised as a shakuhachi player capable of circular breathing and I felt a high degree of achievement in this regard.

However, I had to admit that this wasn't an orthodox way of playing the shakuhachi, and it was a complete enigma to me for a long time how Komusō players in previous centuries managed to play the instrument without, I would assume, having received any training in circular breathing. I talked to people about this and consulted the relevant texts, but I could find no clues to answer my doubts. It seemed as though my breath pilgrimage was set to continue indefinitely.

On the day when my elderly instructor asked me to play a classical piece for him, I didn't have the nerve to play it with recourse to circular breathing. I felt that I needed to play as naturally as possible in front of someone who had succeeded strictly to the orthodox tradition of shakuhachi performance.

On reflection, I felt I'd been lucky to have performed so poorly on that occasion.

An Astonishing Breathing Technique

As I mentioned earlier, I spent the following week receiving lessons from my master, who taught me ten pieces from the large classical repertory handed down over the generations at his temple. I felt my breathing technique was gradually changing as I went through the process of learning the pieces by rote. But starting to work on the pieces again after returning to Tokyo while at the same time renewing my practice of the Missoku technique, I was startled by a new discovery.

One of the most astonishing things about this method of breathing is that it enables you to inhale an enormous amount of air. The more you manage to tilt your pelvis, the more air you're able to inhale. Moreover, there was no longer any sense of having failed to obtain a full intake of breath, and it seemed as if I'd managed to reach full capacity in this regard. Secondly, I had the impression of being able to inhale to the maximum degree in a single instant. And it felt very easy to breathe noiselessly through the nose, perhaps because it had become much easier to do away with the energy in the upper half of my body. Tilting the pelvis has the effect of strongly stabilising the body. A sense of stasis is created as a consequence of the body not moving, of a feeling of stability and of an absence of any breathing noise.

Being able to inhale extremely rapidly meant that aspects of my shakuhachi performance technique that I'd previously found difficult or impossible to execute no longer presented any problem, with the consequence that my power of musical expression increased enormously. I felt that a completely different world had opened up before me when I played pieces handed down among Komusō monks. Sounds emerging from out of a world of total stasis seemed to me as fresh as calligraphic ink falling onto pure white paper.

The gap between one phrase and the next was no longer dependent upon how long it took to breathe, and all kinds of hitherto unknown possibilities opened up before me. What I felt had changed as a consequence of my adoption of this breathing technique was not just my own body but the very world around me. My surroundings seemed to become pervaded by a sense of tranquillity; my body remained totally immobile, meaning that breathing had become an extremely passive action, as if it were wind blowing of its own accord through my body.

It was as if the outlines of the universe had suddenly become clear. As William Blake wrote in *The Marriage of Heaven and Hell*: 'If the doors of perception were cleansed everything would appear to man as it is, infinite' (Blake, 2022, p.11). I realised that Missoku was already something that I had within my immediate grasp.

I often have the opportunity to wear a kimono at my concerts. To ensure that the kimono remains securely in place, it's essential to constantly project one's abdomen and to apply pressure to the kimono on the inside of the obi. The sense of breathing when one does this is exactly what Missoku is all about.

I suddenly realised that this is what I'd been doing all along and that this was what Missoku entailed: a breathing method that one invariably adopts unconsciously whenever one wears a kimono.

The Origins of Missoku

Shakuhachi players in earlier times were able to practise the Missoku technique quite naturally without giving it so much as a second thought. Many classical pieces would have been impossible to perform without mastery of this technique.

The reason it had taken me so long to achieve this realisation was that almost nothing exists in writing about breathing on the shakuhachi. I had avidly searched for documents on the subject of breathing and had read what was available on the Internet and elsewhere, but I'd never found anything in the way of a description of Missoku technique. This wasn't really a question of practitioners deliberately concealing their technique in the belief that it should only be handed down orally to pupils. It was simply because this was a breathing technique that comes naturally to any Japanese person and that isn't particularly out of the ordinary at all.

A breathing technique similar to Missoku may well have been practised in Buddhism too. For example, one of the sutras that conveys the teachings of the Buddha is the *Ānāpānasmṛti Sūtra* (Breath-Mindfulness Discourse). *Ānāpānasmṛti* in Sanskrit or *Ānāpānasati* in Pali denotes breathing as the initial focus for meditation, with the instruction being that one should inhale in short breaths and exhale slowly, allowing only a small amount of breath to escape each time.

At Zen temples, one learns breathing techniques known as *kansoku* and *susoku*. Kansoku is concerned with visualising the breath in order to open the path to enlightenment, in contrast to which susoku involves counting the breath as an ingredient of spiritual training.

The Rinzai sect Zen master, Hakuin (1686–1768), advocated a method of health improvement based on long and slow exhalation of breath. The work in which he expounded such ideas, *Yasen kanna* (Idle Talk on a Night Boat), had a major influence on subsequent generations. In one passage in this work, Hakuin quotes the Daoist philosopher, Zhuangzi, who in one famous passage of his eponymous work wrote that 'The breathing of the true man comes from his heels, while the ordinary man breathes only from his throat' (Muraki, 2003, p.66). Practice of Missoku permits an understanding of what this means. In order to tilt the pelvis and extend the abdomen, one must use the greater psoas muscle, the strength from which is then transmitted from the thighs down to the heels.

It seems to me likely that this breathing method became most strongly advocated as a consequence of its use by Komusō monks when they played the shakuhachi. The shakuhachi is a wind instrument that requires an enormous amount of breath. As a reedless longitudinal end-blown flute, it belongs to the overall category of non-free aerophones that includes the side-blown Western flute, the Japanese *shinobue* and the South American *quena*. In comparison with reed instruments such as the oboe, the clarinet, the saxophone and the Japanese *hichiriki*, reedless instruments are much less efficient and require very large amounts of breath to play. The mouthpiece of the shakuhachi is quite clearly much larger than that of other reedless wind instruments (I shall explain later in Chapter 11 how the size of this mouthpiece makes it possible to generate harmonics). The larger the mouthpiece, the greater the quantity of air required to play the instrument. Reedless instruments are the least efficient of wind instruments, but of all such instruments worldwide it is the shakuhachi that is probably the least efficient of them all in terms of the amount of breath required.

The shakuhachi is an instrument with ancient origins in Central Asia, from where it passed through India and Asia to arrive in Japan during the Nara Period as one of the instruments employed in the early *Gagaku* ensemble. Shakuhachi in pristine condition dating from this period some 1300 or so years ago are preserved to this day in the Shōsōin Imperial Repository.

The shakuhachi comes in a variety of sizes, all structured basically in the same way.

There are stories that the shakuhachi was played by famous figures in the history of Japanese Buddhism such as Shōtoku Taishi and the monk, Ikkyū, but it is not clear how or when the links between the shakuhachi and Buddhism became established. From ancient times through to the medieval period, the shakuhachi appears to have been played by all types of people. The instrument eventually re-emerged onto the stage of history from around the middle of the Edo Period, when it was adopted as a tool for religious training by the itinerant monks known as Komusō belonging to the Fuke sect of Zen Buddhism.

Komusō monks were originally members of the samurai warrior class and no one except Komusō were permitted to play the shakuhachi. As a subsect of the Rinzai school of Zen, the Fuke sect placed great importance upon breathing. Playing the shakuhachi was considered to be a method of training in breathing, and the instrument was thus regarded as a sacred implement to assist a monk in his religious training and practice.

The Fuke sect was abolished in the reforms implemented by the Meiji government in 1871. The monopoly on shakuhachi performance was thus lifted and the instrument became available to anyone who wished to learn it. It was remodelled in various sizes and tunings to enable ensemble performance with other instruments. Nevertheless, the Komusō shakuhachi as previously performed by monks from the Fuke sect continued to survive, albeit in much diminished form.

My main teacher, Katsuya Yokoyama, once told me what an amazing performer his teacher, Watazumidōso, had been. He pointed out how Watazumidōso had mastered the Missoku technique to the extent that you were virtually unaware that he was breathing at all. He marvelled at how this was possible. Watazumidōso is a figure rooted in the past for whom Missoku must have seemed as natural as ordinary breathing. For this reason, he probably thought that there was no need to teach a breathing technique that, for him at least, came so effortlessly and naturally.

Part II

Breathing with the Body and Spirit

Chapter 2

The Missoku Method: Preliminary Stage

Although the bodies of Japanese people have been shaped by the Japanese environment, considerable changes have occurred to the Japanese physique since the Edo Period came to an end a century and a half ago. There's no need to invoke the Edo Period itself to discover how Missoku breathing was performed long ago. It seems likely that people adopted a posture with a tilted pelvis during that era, but Missoku can be executed without adopting such an exaggerated posture. Let's begin by working on an elementary type of Missoku that should come quite naturally to people with modern-day physiques.

Finding One's Own Breathing Method

Try exhaling quite naturally with a breathy sound. Does your abdomen expand or contract as you do so? The answer will depend from the outset on how you breathe normally.

For those whose abdomens expand when breathing in

1. Stop your breath with your abdomen protruding.
2. Inhale with your abdomen protruding and without changing position.

This is what Missoku is all about. You simply need to make sure that you don't change the position of your abdomen. People whose abdomen expands naturally when they exhale are already breathing in a way that gives easy access to Missoku.

For those whose abdomens contract when breathing in

1. Take a deep breath and expand your abdomen to its limit. This should feel as if your abdomen from the navel downward if set to burst. Touch your abdomen with your hands to experience the sensation better.

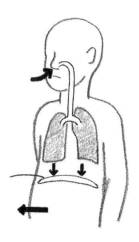

2. Breathe out and then in again whilst keeping your abdomen protruded. Don't actually move anything but maintain the feel of your distended abdomen.

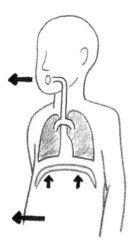

For both breathing types

3. Continue exhaling and inhaling with your abdomen protruding. Keep your abdomen extended when you both inhale and exhale, maintaining the same posture without any movement. It's quite difficult to maintain this posture. When you inhale and exhale there should be absolutely no visible movement of the muscles, with the only movement being that of the diaphragm. In other words, you're making use of the inner muscles that you generally don't use at all.

4. Release your energy. Did you find your body tensing up inside? Release all the tension in your body from your stomach upwards. How about your shoulders, neck, nose and inside the nose? Make sure your legs aren't too tense.

5. Check that the only tension you feel is in the area beneath the navel and in the lower abdomen. It's more difficult to release energy than to insert it. Try focusing on a single point and then releasing energy from everywhere else. Take in a constant succession of very short breaths and you should notice that you're managing to inhale a sufficient quantity of breath in an instant.

6. Pay attention to what's going on around you as you breathe. Your body isn't moving. How do things look around you? For example, the world may seem to have come to a stop. Your senses may be more alert. If you're inside a building, it may appear solid and heavy. Looking outside, the movement of leaves on the trees and the smallest differences between each individual movement may become more perceptible. The sound of the wind and the voices of birds can be heard. All kinds of things can be sensed subtly moving and emitting sounds, creating clearly differentiated, highly complex worlds.

Once you've got this far, you'll have cleared the basics of Missoku breathing.

Advanced Stage

Anyone who wishes to move on to master the Missoku technique on a yet higher level by inhaling a large quantity of air in a single instant and then exhaling it slowly over a long time span needs to adopt the posture used by Japanese people during the Edo Period. This is the advanced stage of Missoku.

1. Fully tilt the pelvis backward.

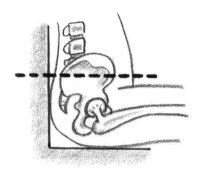

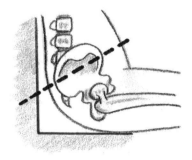

Round your back and shoulders and lean forward with your neck jutting out. Stretch your back from this position.

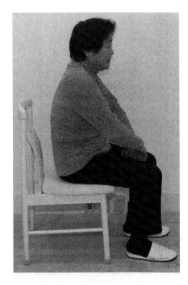

Draw your elbows back and tense your shoulders as if projecting the base of your neck forwards.

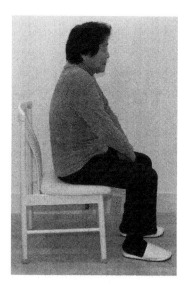

Maintaining balance is difficult without muscular strength but be sure not to make too much effort. Relax your shoulders and thighs in particular.

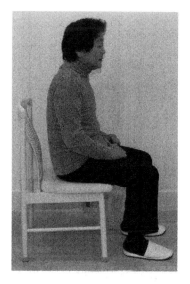

2. Breathe in with your lower abdomen jutting out.
3. Breathe out with your lower abdomen continuing to jut out. Think of a balloon full of water as you push out your lower abdomen yet further.
4. Breathe in again with your lower abdomen still distended. Since there's absolutely no physical movement involved, some people may find it impossible to inhale. They are likely to find it easier if they rotate their shoulders from front to back as they breathe. There should be no need to rotate your shoulders once you've got the hang of it.
5. Release the tension in your body from the toes upwards with the exception of the lower abdomen.

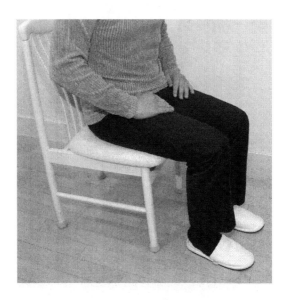

Making a loud noise when you inhale indicates you're putting too much tension into the back of the nose. Breathe as though you have tears in your nose. Release any tension in the narrowest part of the nasal cavity and inhale with the cavity wide open as if from the inner corners of the eyes.

6. Tense your lower abdominal area. It's even better if
    you feel that the tension in your lower abdomen is
    concentrated in the pit of the stomach. You should feel
    the energy not in one particular point but in the whole
    of the lower abdomen, inside the spine and right up the
    sides of the body.

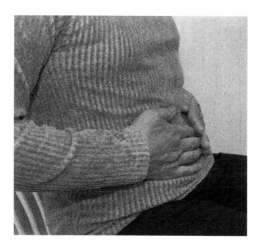

7. Try meditating. Breathe in complete silence without
    even the slightest movement of the body. Take as long
    as possible to breathe out. Try to make yourself invisible

like a *ninja*. Be aware of yourself at one with nature and with your immediate environment. You may get as far as sensing that the barrier between yourself and the outside world has broken down. Sense that you are a vessel permanently open to the world into which air is free to enter and leave. Go further along this path and you'll feel that wind is passing through your body. Change your perspective from a concern with tiny details to a broader picture. For instance, imagine not the veins of a leaf but the tree as a whole, the sky and the external world.

When you've reached this stage, you'll have mastered Missoku.

It might sound difficult, but it boils down to three basic points.

1. Constantly maintain the tension in your abdomen.
2. Tilt your pelvis back further than normal.
3. When you exhale, do so as quietly and as slowly as possible.

The *esoteric breathing* technique of Missoku conveys the impression of mystery and secrecy. I don't know exactly why Watazumidōso gave this technique the name of Missoku, but my personal understanding is that the term has the connotations of hiding the breath during both inhalation and exhalation and conveying the impression to yourself and to others that you aren't breathing at all.

There's no absolutely correct way of practising Missoku. You simply need to experience it for yourself and chart your own feelings. But don't try too hard! Just give it around 15 minutes a day and you should find you'll be able to enjoy the Missoku sensation within a week.

I expect you're accustomed to let out a long, puffy breath when you plop yourself onto the sofa or get into the bath after a hard day at work. This puffy exhalation is an intimation of the Missoku breath present inside our bodies. The pose we adopt when we exhale in this way is the Missoku pose, in which the pelvis is tilted, the abdomen is distended, and energy is released from within.

One particular seated posture often adopted by groups of young people in Japan involves squatting with the elbows placed on the knees. This is a posture that people outside Japan often find it hard to assume; they tend to lose their balance and topple over. Maintaining it for any length of time is difficult. It is in fact a distinctively Japanese posture that involves tilting the pelvis and stabilising both the body and the emotions.

The relative ease with which Japanese people assume this posture indicates that the effects brought about by Missoku are still present within Japanese people's minds and bodies.

Chapter 3

Types of Breathing

	Abdominal breathing	Missoku	Chest breathing	Reverse abdominal breathing
Inhaling	Distended abdomen	Distended abdomen	Distended chest	Distended chest Drawn-in abdomen
Exhaling	Drawn-in abdomen	Abdomen remains distended	Contracted abdomen	Contracted chest Distended chest
Amount of breath	***	****	*	**
Stability (during exhalation)	*	****	**	***
Strength (during exhalation)	****	***	*	**
Release of energy inside the nose	*	****	***	**
Sound	*	****	***	**
	300 – 800 Hz	150 – 400 Hz 2 – 4 kHz	1 – 2 kHz	700 Hz – 1.5 kHz

There are essentially four main methods of breathing, namely abdominal breathing, Missoku, chest breathing and reverse abdominal breathing.

Abdominal breathing and chest breathing are generally well known. Reverse abdominal breathing is an unusual technique that some readers may know from its use in yoga. The method of breathing practised by the Japanese throughout the pre-modern era and still practised today in the traditional arts and martial arts is different from any of the aforementioned techniques. I have chosen to call this traditional Japanese breathing method *Missoku* as suggested by my shakuhachi master.

These four methods are not necessarily the only breathing methods employed today. Other methods may combine different features of these four methods and different individuals may develop their own distinctive breathing methods. Taking the Missoku method on its own, there is a limitless range of variation in the extent to which the pelvis is tilted. Even with abdominal breathing, it's possible to intake a greater amount of air at a quicker speed by tilting the pelvis.

Table 2.1 shows a comparison of the various factors in order to demonstrate the features of breathing with no qualitative judgment implied. For instance, Missoku requires the greatest amount of breath and abdominal breathing the least. On the other hand, chest breathing permits the fastest intake of breath and is appropriate for singers wishing to project their voices.

Abdominal Breathing

Abdominal breathing is in a certain sense a very natural breathing method. When you breathe the lungs expand, pressing down on the diaphragm and in turn on the organs in the abdomen. This naturally results in the abdomen distending outward. Drawing in the abdomen during exhalation raises the internal organs and then the diaphragm, as a result of which the lungs contract and air is expelled. This is a rational method of breathing that involves the whole body.

Missoku

The main feature of Missoku is the posture adopted during exhalation. Breath is expelled with the abdomen distended in a posture different from that which one would naturally assume.

Chest Breathing

Chest breathing involves a variety of postures and abdominal states that differ from one person to another, the common feature of which is expansion of the chest when one inhales, and contraction when one exhales. The diaphragm hardly moves vertically at all. This is an easy breathing method that entails little effort.

Reverse Abdominal Breathing

This method involves contracting the abdomen when you breathe, an action that inevitably involves expanding the chest. As with chest breathing when you breathe out, you contract the chest while at the same time expanding the abdomen. The main difference between this method and Missoku is that the body moves. Beginners in yoga are likely to have found it difficult initially to relax when taking a full breath. It may feel like you're moving organs inside your body that you don't normally move.

Features of Each Breathing Method

Quantity of Breath

Quantity of breath refers to the volume of air that we introduce into our lungs.

In the case of chest breathing, the diaphragm doesn't move that much. Since it involves merely expanding the lungs, this method entails the smallest intake of breath. A greater quantity of air is introduced in the reverse abdominal breathing method, which involves drawing down the abdomen. Even larger quantities of breath can be taken in through the use of abdominal breathing and Missoku, which entail expanding the abdomen. The main difference between Missoku and abdominal breathing lies in the posture adopted. In the case of Missoku, the pelvis is tilted backwards, a movement that entails a widening of the abdomen and a further lowering of the diaphragm. This makes it possible to expand the lungs and increase breath intake.

Raising and lowering the pelvis while practising abdominal breathing maximises breath intake. A rapid intake of breath with a lowering of the pelvis followed by an exhaled puff of breath as the pelvis is raised entails the same inhalation as in the case of Missoku. Furthermore, use of the surface muscles to achieve full exhalation makes it possible to expel even more air than with Missoku. This is not possible, however, without extensive, conscious physical movement.

Stability

Stability depends on ensuring a smooth quantity of air. Missoku is the most stable method of breathing because it merely involves pulling up the diaphragm and making use of the inner muscles and with no exertion required apart from this. In contrast, abdominal breathing involves expelling air through movement of the abdominal and chest muscles and makes it difficult to achieve stability. The posture employed in reverse abdominal breathing creates stability in terms of the amount of air exhaled. But drawing in the abdomen when inhaling results in physical movement.

Effort

Effort here refers to the strength expended when exhaling. The greatest amount of effort is required in the abdominal breathing method in which a large quantity of air is expelled through muscular exertion. The least effort is required by abdominal breathing, which involves intake of a relatively small amount of air. In this respect, Missoku, with its very large intake of air, and reverse abdominal breathing, lags behind abdominal breathing.

Speed

Since it entails merely dropping the diaphragm, Missoku is the fastest method of inhaling, followed in this respect by chest breathing, which involves simply taking in air into the lungs, with their relatively high position inside the body. Next in terms of speed comes the reverse abdominal breathing method in which the abdomen is retracted during inhalation. Abdominal breathing is a rational method of breathing, but since it involves use of muscles to take in air to a low position in the body, it requires movement of the whole body and is thus the slowest method.

Relaxing Tension inside the Nose

Relaxing tension inside the noise means releasing energy from the neck upward. In the case of abdominal breathing, tension is applied through use of the muscles throughout the body when breathing. The pressure and effort involved affect the narrow space inside the nostrils, meaning that tension is generated inside the nose. Chest breathing entails a relatively low amount of breath and effort and thus makes it easy to relax tension. Once the inner muscles are developed, lowering the pelvis enables a high overall level of stability even when there is no tension in the upper body. Smooth inhalation is thus possible without having to put any effort into breathing and facilitates relaxation from the neck upward.

Sound

The easily accessible pitch range and tone of a person's voice differs depending upon the tilt of the pelvis and the method of breathing.

The tone in the case of Missoku tends to be somewhat muffled. The pitch range lies between 150 and 400 hertz, corresponding to the tessitura of a baritone. Chest breathing is suited to the alto range of between 300 and 800 hertz. The reverse chest breathing method is suited to the higher mezzo-soprano range of between 700 and 1500 hertz. Chest breathing is suited to the even higher range of the soprano of between 1000 and 2000 hertz. Missoku also facilitates production of extremely high pitches in the range of three to four kilohertz. The sound in this case is accompanied by a significant noise element. I intend to expand on this in Chapter 11, but the essential point is that overtones begin to emerge at this point.

Looking at Table 2.1 at the beginning of this chapter, it's clear that Missoku is the most effective method in terms of quantity of breath, stability, effort when exhaling, speed of inhalation and relaxation of tension, although this doesn't mean that it is the best option for everyone. For instance, reverse abdominal breathing is scarcely ever used in the context of everyday life, but because it's an unnatural method, it places a considerable burden on the body and helps to strengthen one's muscles. It's used in activities such as Tai Chi, yoga and pilates specifically to strengthen the inner organs and muscles.

Missoku is of considerable benefit to shakuhachi players, but we have to change over to abdominal breathing when we want to produce an explosive sound following a crescendo. When exhaling, very strong force can be projected by mobilising the abdominal muscles and tightening them from the diaphragm. On the other hand, Missoku is ideal when one wants to produce a long pianissimo note.

With abdominal breathing it's difficult to maintain the body in a fixed position and exhale in a stable manner. Shakuhachi players are able to expand their expressive range by making free use of both Missoku and abdominal breathing.

Abdominal breathing is the method generally used by classical singers. It enables them to project a clear tone and is suited to performance of Western music. But there are some sopranos who deliberately plump for chest breathing, in which case both the amount of breath and the effort required in breathing are relatively small. This is because voice projection is facilitated by lifting up the chest and raising the pelvis.

Focusing on parts rather than on the whole isn't a good idea at all. For instance, you might try to repair a fishing rod by strengthening it in one place only to find that it soon snaps somewhere else. The point is that the rod is flexible because it maintains its overall strength. But people involved in sports these days tend to focus specifically on strengthening their thigh muscles, their upper body or some other specific area. This has resulted in an increase in the number of athletes experiencing torn muscles.

Rather than attempting to master a method of breathing as rapidly as possible by working on one specific area, the best idea is to work on it naturally while breathing in the usual way. Breathing shouldn't be thought of as a means of cultivating the body. The aim should be to discover a natural and healthy type of breathing fully compatible with one's own body and to establish a relaxed and composed physical constitution.

Chapter 4.

Posture and Position of the Pelvis

Why do Japanese people today breathe from the chest? They inevitably breathe from the chest because they have forgotten the traditional Missoku technique but nor have they fully mastered the Western technique of abdominal breathing either. Most people these days naturally inflate their abdomen when they inhale but retract it when they exhale.

Try tilting your pelvis down and taking in a deep breath without putting any effort into it. Although it's easy to inflate the abdomen, it's difficult to retract it and only a small quantity of air gets expelled when one does so. This means that it's only possible to intake a small amount of air on the next breath and that the air goes no further than the chest. Without putting a lot of effort into it, one's breath gets shallower and shallower. The basic posture when we breathe involves tilting the pelvis. The Missoku method makes use of the deep muscles, which maintain the expansion of the abdomen when we breathe out and which lift up the diaphragm as if detaching it from its original position. Next, try raising your pelvis up straight. I expect you'll find it much easier now to retract your abdomen. On the other hand, no doubt you'll also find that inhaling with your abdomen inflated is tricky without a bit of effort. This is because the raised pelvis posture is the one we adopt when we exhale.

Most people in Western countries have their pelvis raised when they assume a natural posture. The basic posture in the West tends to be the exhaling posture with the pelvis raised, with the outer muscles of the body being used to inhale. This doesn't involve any particular training and the muscular strength required for this purpose is obtained naturally by breathing like this on an everyday basis.

I expect most of us when we were children got told off by our parents for not sitting up straight when sitting in a chair or for slouching when we should be standing up straight with our chest out. Indeed, it's common to see adults slouching on their seats on the train on the way home after a tiring day's work at the office.

The lifestyles of Japanese people have become increasingly Westernised and it's by no means unusual for Japanese homes these days not to have a single traditional style room with tatami flooring. For most Japanese people, the easiest and most natural posture is one with our pelvis lowered. It's often said that many Japanese people today have drooping bottoms, but what this means is not that the flesh on their bottoms is drooping but rather that they're allowing their pelvis to collapse downward. The reason for this is that they no longer lead a lifestyle in which they have to keep their pelvis in a raised position, and it's because of their posture that they find it so hard to practise abdominal breathing in a natural manner.

This may seem a pity from the standpoint of a Western aesthetic or style. Moreover, one has to consciously work on training the muscles in order to practise abdominal breathing. It's not possible to practise abdominal breathing effectively without being aware of the position of one's pelvis before making a start with training.

From this perspective, Missoku can be regarded as a natural method of breathing. It's just that it has become difficult for Japanese people to breathe in this way because raising the pelvis has come to be regarded as the key to a supposedly correct posture. This is because Japanese people tend to be encouraged to practise abdominal breathing because of the ongoing Westernisation of the Japanese lifestyle, which has resulted in a deterioration in the muscles used for Missoku breathing.

If your pelvis is lowered or if you're breathing from the chest, this means that you haven't yet moved on to abdominal breathing. But with training, it should be easy to learn the Missoku method. It's possible to master the initial stages of this method as I outlined at the start of Chapter 2 without too much effort.

The Physical Constitution That Makes It Difficult to Practise Missoku

Abdominal breathing involves raising the pelvis and using the whole body. Breathing in this way requires the physique, position of the pelvis and thick surface muscles possessed by Westerners. In contrast, Missoku involves raising and lowering the diaphragm using the deep muscles and without any movement of the body. Most Japanese people today are unable to practise Missoku; they practise chest breathing in a way that makes it impossible for them to move on to abdominal breathing. I'd like to consider now the nature of the changes that this has brought about in Japanese people's bodies.

Shallowness of Breath

Watching young people recently, I've noticed that they tend to breathe with their mouth open. I get the impression that they are no longer able to breathe through the nose. I imagine this is because their weak deep muscles and abdominal muscles mean that they are practising chest breathing and raising and lowering their shoulders.

Breathing through the mouth dries out the palate and places strain on the throat. Chest breathing whereby short, shallow breaths are taken through the mouth is the breathing method that involves the smallest intake of air and, indeed, poses a risk to life itself.

It's the parasympathetic nervous system that exercises control over sleep and rest. Fast, shallow breathing irritates the parasympathetic nervous system with the consequence that mind and body are in a constant state of activity, resulting in a build-up of stress. It seems to me that Japanese society as a whole has lost the ability to breathe deeply and that this has resulted in the formation of a physical constitution characterised by stress and tension.

Breathing deeply and slowly is thought to have various beneficial effects. In his book on breathing, *Kokyū no shikumi* (How Breathing Works), Ichirō Kita enumerates these as follows:

1. Wellness generated by activation of serotonin nerves.
2. Regulation of the circulatory organs, the endocrine system and immunity functions and maintenance of homeostasis by balancing the autonomic nervous system.
3. Recovery from fatigue through activation of gas exchange.
4. Encouraging digestion and decomposition through simulation of the abdominal cavity (Kita, 2005, p.197).
5. Enhancing conscious awakening.
6. Inhibiting pain.
7. Supporting muscular activity (Kita, 2005, p.191).
8. Production of alpha waves to encourage relaxation and concentration.

These are just some of the beneficial effects of breathing. Since breathing quite literally makes it possible to change one's body, we need to work on breathing slowly and deeply.

Poor Posture

One often sees people sticking out or splaying their legs when seated in a train. My reaction to this used to be that it was just bad manners, but I've come to realise recently that it's a consequence of a decline in their muscular strength. Even with a lowered pelvis it's possible to keep one's legs closed as long as one has enough muscular strength, but some people clearly find it difficult to do this because of the weakness in their muscles between the lower abdomen and the thighs.

When attending a concert, I've often noticed Japanese performers sitting with their legs open and crossed on the stage while waiting their turn to perform. This is a posture that no Western performer would assume.

There are many people who would topple over unless they stood firm in a rocking train or would immediately fall over if they lost their footing on a hillside. But these days such people are no longer just elderly people but also youngsters in their teens and twenties. This provides evidence of the decay in Japanese people's hips and lower abdomen and in the muscles in the back of their feet that they use to stand and walk. This decay is closely related to the fact that Japanese people have become unable to practise the Missoku style of breathing.

Increase in Preparatory Movement

Generating a movement by rebounding from a preparatory movement has not traditionally been common among Japanese people. Once they reach their teens, when standing, sitting or opening a door, children have tended to avoid such preparatory movements. But these days perfectly ordinary everyday movements tend to be accompanied by preparatory movements often with accelerated motion.

Uniform motion unaccompanied by rebound or acceleration is hard to control without physical stability and considerable muscular strength. When studying the Ogasawara school of traditional etiquette, otherwise perfectly fit men may find themselves out of breath when they practise standing up or sitting down smoothly and quietly. Movements that would have seemed absolutely normal for Japanese people in the past now demand enormous effort from people today.

In *Kendō*, the Japanese art of swordsmanship, it has become customary for practitioners to lower or raise their bamboo swords by rebounding from a prior step as in fencing. We're accustomed to watching historical dramas in which two samurai face one another motionlessly, as if time had stopped, with their swords interlocked and then, in a flash with no preparatory motion whatsoever, one of them is struck down. There are few cases where image and reality are so different.

The physical stillness engendered by Missoku makes it possible to move without any preparatory movement. This is a consequence of changing the way one breathes.

Nervousness

Japanese people tend to get nervous or experience stage fright in various situations. One of the reasons for this seems to me to lie in the practice of chest breathing. Not being able to breathe slowly generates a negative synergistic effect.

Becoming tense and nervous in certain situations results in shorter and shallower breaths. Taking in a deeper breath requires more physical energy. Neither the chest nor the abdomen expand, meaning that one becomes less and less able to breathe with an accompanying strong increase in tension. It thus becomes increasingly difficult to do something that we normally do with no problem whatsoever. This vicious circle gives yet further stimulus to the phenomenon of stage fright.

Taking in a single deep breath has the effect of breaking this vicious circle. But the problem when trying to breathe deeply from a state in which we take short and shallow breaths is that the pelvis is in a raised position as if standing to attention. The raised pelvis position is the position we adopt when breathing out. Considerable muscular strength is required in order to take a deep breath from this position. The only way to cope with this is either to strengthen the muscles or, conversely, to lower the pelvis. It's a question of mastering either abdominal breathing or Missoku.

Start by tilting your pelvis. Exhale through the nose while slowly raising your upper body from this position, then take in a deep breath. It has been proved that proper breathing has the effect of stabilising the body, inducing relaxation and heightening concentration. What this means is that physical tension results in mental tension. Try it for yourself! Tilt your pelvis, breathe out slowly and then take in a deep breath in nerve-racking situations, even if your nerves are already on edge.

Part III

The Japanese Body

Chapter 5

The Origins of Missoku

Let's examine in more detail why and how the Missoku breathing technique arose in Japan. The main factor that explains why the Japanese people acquired this breathing technique is surely the natural environment. Three quarters of Japan's national territory is occupied by hills and mountains, meaning that there is a proliferation of steep slopes. Furthermore, Japan has a mild climate, soft soil and a proliferation of plants all over the country.

The combination of factors such as (a) the hilly and mountainous character of the national terrain; (b) the many steep slopes; (c) the mild climate and soft soil; and (d) the proliferation of trees and plants and other such natural conditions has meant that land throughout Japan has presented a natural environment that offers extremely poor footing. Steep slopes and soft soil mean that it's difficult to stand up straight and that people have to bend their legs and lower their centre of gravity. Moreover, since most native Japanese trees are deciduous and broad-leaved, their leaves fall with the arrival of winter, making the ground even more unstable to walk over.

In Japan, historically, hunting and gathering was the general means of subsistence until the emergence of rice cultivation, but this did not involve people exploiting prairies and other such wide-open spaces. On the contrary, hunting and gathering was restricted to the areas between mountains and forests and in the midst of the leaves fallen from broad-leaved trees.

Movement in places with extensive plant life tends to be accompanied by sound. In order to suppress sound so that animals would be unaware of the hunter's presence, the hunter would have to maintain a lowered posture, thus enabling him to leap out onto the attack at the right moment.

Working Environment

After the method of rice cultivation had been introduced into Japan from the neighbouring countries, paddy fields were created all over the country, taking advantage of the mild, temperate climate. Work in the paddy fields places a considerable burden on the legs and the back and movement is difficult without coordination between the hips and the upper body.

In his book *Kūkan no nihon bunka* (Japanese Culture of Space), the French cultural anthropologist, Augustin Berque, writes something similar:

'Low-lying, flat ground makes up 13 percent of the national territory, fairly high tableland 12 percent, and various types of mountain-foot regions 3 percent, constituting together 28 percent of the whole national territory. A half of this land is under cultivation, and a third of this is given over to paddy fields.' (Berque, 1994, p.140.)

He then goes on to explain:

'Early on in the Nara Period, a single hectare of paddy would produce an average of between 0.9 tons in poor quality fields to 1.6 tons in better quality fields. By the 18th century yield per hectare had risen to between 2.0 and 2.7 more tons, figures superior to those obtained in most third-world countries today (Yield per hectare in India in 1978 was 2 tons and in Brazil 1.3 tons).' (Berque, 1994, p.149.)

This means that the yield per unit of area was higher during the Nara and Heian periods than in Brazil in the second half of the twentieth century. It's not clear why Japanese people managed to work so intensively and efficiently, but it is clear nevertheless that from ancient times down to the present-day, workers in the paddy fields have been obliged, because of the need to secure their footing on unstable ground, to work with bent knees. The legs and lower backs of people working while maintaining such a posture with the pelvis tilted backwards would inevitably have been strengthened.

Factor (e) was thus the existence of a working environment in the form of rice cultivation, which stimulated strengthening of the muscles of the lower back and legs.

Everyday Living Environment

Similar conditions to those applicable to the working environment applied in the case of the everyday living environment too. Factor (f) is the Japanese custom of sitting on tatami mats on the floor, with a standard seated posture and the effort required to stand up from this posture, while factor (g) is related to the custom of wrapping an obi sash around the hips and adopting a natural posture with the lower abdomen held firmly in place.

In his book *Isu to Nihonjin no karada* (Chairs and the Japanese Body), Hidemasa Yatabe writes:

'The Japanese are easily influenced by other cultures, and in this respect are no different now from how they were in the past. But seen from a long-term historical perspective, for instance, at the time when trade with continental Asia fell into decline and a distinctively Japanese culture emerged, chairs disappeared totally from the court and from temples and almost all Japanese people went back to sitting on the floor. Similarly, when the Tokugawa government closed the country and placed restrictions on trade with the West, the chairs and beds that had been fashionable in some quarters during the Muromachi Period fell into total disuse and people returned to sitting directly on the floor on tatami mats.' (Yatabe, 2004, p.52.)

Yatabe gives several reasons for this, specifically the outlook that determines the features of Japanese living spaces, the underlying influence of Zen Buddhism, and the physical sensation of placing the centre of gravity in the abdomen.

At present in Japan there are plenty of residences with no tatami rooms that consist entirely of Western style rooms. More and more children are being raised in such environments, and it seems that Japanese people have finally become accustomed to sitting on chairs. But nevertheless, it's fascinating to see that when people gather for a party in someone's home and the atmosphere becomes more and more informal, it's common for them to move off the sofa and sit on the floor instead. This is something not often seen in other countries and implies that the posture that Japanese people tend to assume when they want to relax is, as in the past, that of sitting on the floor.

Life spent sitting on tatami mats with no back support involves extensive use of the muscles from the lower abdomen down through the legs. Everyone from the young to the elderly, whenever they stood up or sat down, used to perform squats similar to those of a gymnast hundreds of times a day. Everyday customs practised by people over many centuries no doubt had the effect of fundamentally changing the Japanese physique.

Most Japanese people these days have had little experience of wrapping an obi sash around their waist beneath the navel. In his book *Shintai kankaku o torimodosu* (Regaining Bodily Sensation), Takashi Saitō writes as follows:

'I recently had the experience of sharing lodgings with young men in their twenties, and one thing in particular surprised me. I noticed that when they put on yukata gowns in the hotel where we were staying, they wrapped the sash around the pit of the stomach, that is to say the thinner area of the waist between the chest and the stomach. In earlier times in Japan, attaching the obi in a position above the navel would have been restricted in the case of males to children. I was astonished to see full-bodied young men attach their obi in a position associated with children with no second thoughts.' (Saitō, 2000, p.25.)

The position in which one attaches an obi is closely connected with the awareness of one's own body. Saitō expresses his concern that this reflects a regression in the physical notion of the waist and hips. I would agree with this, although with the reservation that young people, once they have worn a kimono four or five times, tend to revert to the correct, traditional method of wear. This might be attributed to habituation or to restriction on free movement, but there is more to it than this.

Anyone who knows how to wear a kimono correctly will, in the case of a man, place the obi around the hipbones, and, in the case of woman, place the cord that adjusts the length of the kimono prior to attachment of the obi, around the hipbones. Once the lower abdomen is secured, one's focus moves to this part of the body. Saito goes on to say:

'The obi resists expansion of the abdomen. This resistance exerted by the obi doesn't suppress strength but rather has the effect of drawing forth strength from the abdomen. The obi has the effect of drawing the lower abdomen forward, which then tightens the pelvis.'

The obi thus functions to extend the abdomen quite naturally. This is the basic pose required by the Missoku breathing technique, which implies that mastery of Missoku enables the correct wearing of a kimono. Even in the case of young people, the fact that the more they wear a kimono the less likely it is to become disarrayed indicates that they have unconsciously begun to practise Missoku breathing. Traditional costume in the form of the kimono and obi provides a vivid indication of how Japanese people used to breathe and of how people today should breathe. The kimono will never fall into disarray if one presses with the abdomen against the inside of the obi and places the kimono beneath it. In contrast, many non-Japanese find that, however often they put on a kimono, it always falls into disarray. No matter how demurely they move, the practice of abdominal breathing means that the abdomen is constricted, resulting in the obi and kimono falling out of place in respect to each other.

The obi is similar in shape to a belt, but the two items clearly function in a totally different way. A belt is placed around the waist above the pelvis in the form of a small band in order to hold up one's trousers. On the other hand, an obi has the function of holding the kimono between itself and the abdomen to ensure that the kimono remains stable and in place. This means that it's necessary to extend the abdomen when one puts on an obi, whereas a belt is fixed around the pelvis irrespective of the state of the body.

Such environmental factors have resulted in the distinctive posture and physical properties of Japanese people.

Posture and Physical Properties

Conditions of the natural environment have thus resulted in the adoption as a matter of course of a posture that involves lowering the hips, tilting the pelvis and bending the knees. Adoption of this posture in everyday life has resulted in the natural acquisition of a method of breathing that involves tilting the pelvis and extending the lower abdomen. Once this posture has been acquired and Missoku breathing is practised, these physical properties are maintained and strengthened within the framework of everyday life.

Breathing and the environment have thus mutually reinforced each other. This applies to the Japanese approach to the floor and to the culture of the kimono. Since the practice of Missoku results in maintenance of physical stability and repose, this posture is ideal for producing sounds and conveys a sense of tranquillity in which inadvertent body and hand gestures appear unsettling.

Children are unable to control their breathing, bodily gestures and voices. As they grow up, they gradually become able to control them in a calm and collected manner. As a consequence of growing up while breathing in this way they develop extremely strong muscular strength on the outside and inside of their legs and hips. Lifestyles that make it possible to maintain such muscular strength have slowly come to fruition over many centuries.

Chapter 6

The Gestures of Japanese People

Working and walking with one's hips tilted back requires considerable muscular strength. We tend to think that this posture is restricted these days to athletes in a small number of sports, but it is frequently encountered in the traditional Japanese performing arts too.

Take the example of the folk stage art of *Hayachine Kagura* in Iwate Prefecture. An elderly man named Sanbasō appears on the stage and moves around in an entertaining manner. A clown then appears and copies the old man's gestures, gradually including a variety of errors. Sanbasō begins to dance on one leg after attaching the other leg to a piece of string attached to his hips, whereupon the clown, who needs to be particularly skilful, begins to dance in the same way with one leg placed inside the neckband of his costume. This requires enormous flexibility of the joints as the clown jumps up and down, along with vast reserves of strength.

In the Kagura performed in the village of Shība in Miyazaki Prefecture, the performer chases his rival in a posture similar to that of *sumo* wrestlers when they stamp on the ground alternately with their right and left feet. This continues for more than ten minutes at a fast tempo in a posture that has become impossible for those of us living in the big cities to assume today.

Such manifestations of the traditional performing art of Kagura exist throughout Japan. According to Tomiko Kojima, an ethnomusicologist who has conducted extensive research on Kagura, performers constantly tilt their pelvis and stand on their big toe joints. Their knees and ankles are flexible, and they place their heels just above the ground so that they can transfer their centre of gravity onto either foot. They take in long breaths and are skilled at breathing. These dynamic and robust performing arts from Japan's rural, mountainous areas are rooted in the traditional use of the body on a daily basis.

Beginning with basic movements and gestures, let's take a look now at how these physical states, such as a posture with the pelvis tilted and the knees bent, the Missoku breathing technique and muscular strength, actually developed.

Standing: Location of the Centre of Gravity

Watching the actors in a performance in the *Kabuki* theatre, there are various things one notices apart from the quality of the play itself. One of the most conspicuous features of the most illustrious Kabuki actors is their posture. They manage to convey an overwhelming stage presence, but they stand in a pose that differs slightly from that adopted by us today. Their posture cannot be clearly seen when they appear on stage in a long kimono, but this difference in posture is immediately evident when they turn up the hem of the kimono and appear in the guise of the ordinary Edo townsman. The typical pose is slightly bowlegged with the feet turned outward. This pose is a long way from the pose that typifies the Western aesthetic with the legs straight, the abdomen raised and the shoulders thrown back, but it looks most impressive all the same.

The main difference between these two poses lies in the positioning of the centre of gravity. In the case of the Western posture with the pelvis raised, the centre of gravity is set on both feet or somewhere between them. As anyone is aware when they strike a pose other than that of standing bolt upright to attention, in the Western standing pose the centre of gravity allows for easy and extreme movement. In contrast, Japanese people used to stand with their knees slightly bent and their pelvis lowered. But since the upper torso does not lean forward, the centre of gravity is located slightly behind the space between the legs.

There's someone else I'd like to mention in connection with the standing pose, namely the great exponent of traditional Japanese dance, Han Takehara. Her principal characteristic on the stage was her standing pose. As well as being a wonderful dancer, she stood on the stage in a manner unique to herself. Although she bent her knees, she supported the weight of her body by drawing one leg back, meaning that her centre of gravity was placed on the leg positioned half a step behind the other leg. As a result, she would stretch her pelvis with the knees slightly extended, with a high centre of gravity and her feet looking elegant and slender.

Leading dancers among her contemporaries seem in contrast to be bending their hips and knees, making the lower half of their body look shorter than it really is. One can conclude from this that, leaving aside any value judgments, Han Takehara was responsible for reforming and modernising the genre of traditional Japanese dance.

The distinctive standing pose adopted by Japanese people gave rise to the distinctive manner in which they move. This was the natural pose adopted by the Japanese over the centuries until they were forced into adopting a Western posture and it's the pose that I referred to in detail when discussing the method of Missoku. This pose is clearly evident in photographs of Japanese people dating from the Meiji era.

A seller of potted plants photographed by Hugues Krafft, from *Bonjūru Japon* (1882–83).

Walking: Nanba-aruki

I was once brought up with a start upon encountering a passage in a book entitled *Dentō to danzetsu* (Tradition and Rupture) by Tetsuji Takechi in which he states that Japanese people were originally unable to run in the way that this word is interpreted in the West.

It was the Kabuki actor, Ichikawa Sadanji II, who in 1880 first performed the action of tilting the body to turn a corner on the Kabuki stage. At the first performance of a play entitled *Banchō sarayashiki* (The Dish Mansion in Banchō) in 1916, Sadanji made his appearance by running with his body bent forward along the *hanamichi* passage through the auditorium onto the stage, in a motion that would have astonished and excited the audience because such an action had until then been unknown in Japan. Sadanji studied in England and is said to have incorporated Western style movements into the Kabuki theatre.

73

How then did Japanese people run or walk up until that time? They appear to have walked in a manner known in Japanese as *nanba-aruki*. This involves walking without twisting the body in such a way that the left leg and the left arm and then the right leg and the right arm move forward together. One sometimes sees young children and elderly people walking like this even today in Japan.

This was a natural way of walking if one considers the physical features of the Japanese. If the sacrum is tilted, the centre of gravity moves backward and it becomes relatively difficult to bring forward the arm and the leg on opposite sides of the body. This is immediately evident if one attempts to walk with the pelvis tilted backward. But although it's possible to walk smoothly transferring the centre of gravity from right to left, it's difficult to accelerate. Transfer of the centre of gravity is essential in order to run fast. Hiroshi Itō, who retired after holding the Asian sprint record with a time of just over ten seconds for the 100-meter sprint has stated that the pelvis of ethnic Japanese tends to be located much further back than in people of other ethnicities. The pelvis of people of Black ethnicity especially tends to tilt forward, which is key to their being able to run so fast. In contrast, since the pelvis of Japanese people tends to tilt backward, Itō made a valiant effort to conquer this disability by changing the position of his pelvis. It was this effort that enabled him to beat the Asian sprint record.

Let's take a look at the benefits of the nanba-aruki method of walking, a method unsuited to acceleration, as we have seen. One of its benefits lies in stability and the fact that there is little movement of the centre of gravity.

Walking in the manner of people of European descent with the pelvis raised means that the centre of gravity moves from the right leg to the left leg. This constant forward transfer in the centre of gravity is what propels the walker forward. Since the centre of gravity is moved entirely from one leg to the other, the position itself tends to be highly unstable. However, in the case of nanba-aruki, the centre of gravity is located in the hips rather than constantly being brought forward, meaning that it is never placed on a single leg. When the left leg is placed in front of the right leg, the centre of gravity is not fully transferred from the right leg to the left leg. This means that its position is constant, thus making it possible to walk in a stable manner.

This manner of walking may have arisen to make it easier to walk on unstable ground. One has merely to imagine walking on a mountain slope, in a paddy field or in a children's swimming pool in which the water comes up to one's waist. If we today try walking in our normal manner with opposite arms and legs moving forward, we're likely to find ourselves falling over or being pushed back by the water and will find it more difficult than we thought to move forward. However, with the nanba-aruki method we feel stable and can move forward against the water. It's not possible to work on mountain slopes, in paddy fields or on any unstable ground unless one employs the nanba-aruki method.

The other point is the speed of movement, that is to say the fact that there's no need for any preparatory movement. In his book *Kobujutsu ni manabu shintai sōhō* (Physical Techniques to be Learned from the Ancient Martial Arts), Yoshinori Kōno refers to use of the body without any need for preparatory movement such as twisting or bending. The principle involved here would appear to be that the joints are extended when the pelvis is raised, resulting in separation of the chest from the hips and a double action whereby, whenever one does something, the hips are moved before the chest moves. In contrast, the chest and the hips are joined together when the pelvis is tilted. Indeed, one might say that the body as a whole forms a single unit. This means that a single action is all that's required when performing a movement of some kind and that there's no need for any preparatory movement. One consequence of this is the acquisition of speed. It would seem that a vast reserve of strength emerges when the chest and the hips form a single unit, but to the extent that the pelvis is tilted, strength conversely ebbs away and the whole body is relaxed, meaning that strength can be transmitted rapidly.

Movements and the Tools of Daily Life

Squatting
Squatting with the hips thoroughly lowered is a posture that people outside Japan rarely assume, although in Japan it was a common, everyday posture until fairly recently. When taking a break from physical labour, Japanese people would customarily assume a squatting posture. This posture used to be common in children's games. For instance, the skipping rope jump known as Postman (yūbin'ya-san) involves jumping up each time from a squatting position and requires an enormous outlay of energy. This used to be a common game played by girls. Traditional Japanese style toilets also used to require their users to squat.

Pulling: Planes, Saws and Carving Knives
Tools that call for their users to adopt a posture with a tilted pelvis include carpenters' tools such as planes and saws. The Western saw is used by pushing forward. It's generally made of steel so that it doesn't bend, and the cut itself is inflexible. Japanese carpenters, however, work with the pelvis tilted, meaning that they are relatively weak when they need to push the saw forward. Their effort therefore goes into pulling rather than pushing. Such physical conditions have given rise to the distinctive type of saw used in Japan.

An elderly woodcutter, from the Morse Collection
Hyakunen mae no Nihon (Japan One Hundred Years Ago).

When I was a child, I learnt from my father how to use the wooden pestle and mortar employed to mash yams and *miso*. If you put a lot of strength into it, it's hard to retain your balance and the contents spill out of the mortar. Parents used to teach their children that the way to perform this operation smoothly is to adopt a stable posture with the hips lowered.

Although Japanese carving knives come in many varieties depending on their intended use, they are basically the same as the knives used in the West. But differences arise when it comes to how they are used. For example, in Japan, when cutting up or thinly slicing fish, it's the custom to draw the knife inward rather than pushing it outward, with extensive use being made of the tip of the blade, which requires adoption of a stable posture with the hips lowered. In the West on the other hand, the motion generally involves carving by pushing from above, making skilful use of bodily weight and the weight of the knife.

Such differences arise to some extent from differences in food materials and culinary techniques, but the action of drawing the knife toward you rather than pushing it away from you with the pelvis in an upright position results in an unstable centre of gravity, meaning that pushing forward to carve is the more natural gesture.

Pulling: Hand Cars and Rickshaws

Wheelbarrows are a common sight these days, but they were only introduced into Japan relatively recently. Before then it was customary to pull rather than to push, using a two- wheeled handcart pulled from in front.

As becomes clear if one tries to use such a device, it's extremely difficult to pull in a position with the pelvis raised. In physical education classes at school, it used to be common to work on strengthening the legs and back by pulling forward a roller of the type used to level ground. Pupils would be told to direct their strength from the pelvis and not to straighten their legs. Conversely, by tilting the pelvis backward and adopting a posture with the hips lowered it becomes difficult to push. When pushing a wheelbarrow forward it's necessary to straighten one's back and maintain a high centre of gravity in order to apply one's body weight to the forward motion.

Shouldering: Mikoshi Shrines

My father was born in Anpachi in Gifu Prefecture, where shrine festivals involve thirty men running at a fast speed carrying an extremely heavy portable shrine on their shoulders. He recalled that they are able to do this without even the slightest vertical movement. Because the shrine is so heavy, to move so fast would be impossible if it were to bob up and down. But when a local young man who has left the neighbourhood to study or work in a big city came back home for a while and joined in the band holding up the shrine, it all went awry. Balance was lost and the shrine weighed down on everyone, with the consequence that all the participants ended up with sore shoulders.

My father's recollection dated from the immediate pre-war or post-war years. This was an era when the pelvis of most Japanese people tended to tilt backward and people were able to run with heavy weights on their shoulders but without any vertical movement. Thereafter lifestyles in the major cities became increasingly Westernised, resulting in the gradual adoption of a pose with the pelvis maintained upright.

It seems quite likely that changes came about thereafter in the features of portable *mikoshi* shrines and other items that play a part in festivals, with them either falling into disuse or becoming much smaller and lighter in weight. The *mikoshi* that feature in the Sanja-matsuri festival held annually in the Asakusa district of Tokyo are carried while being moved up and down in a two-beat rhythm with cries of *'seiya!'* or *'soiya!'* Up to around eighty years ago though, the cry was apparently *'wasshoi!'*, as is general in Japanese when carrying something particularly heavy.

In earlier times the *mikoshi* were heavier than they are now and the men who bore them on their shoulders had sturdy physiques in the traditional Edo manner. The repetitive exclamatory cry was therefore associated with heavy loads. Someone during the early post-war years seems to have thought it would be a good idea to replace this cry with cries associated with lightness and speed, and this soon became the standard. It is indeed easier to carry a *mikoshi* in a high position with the pelvis raised, and this is the posture more appropriate when carrying it at a rapid speed through the narrow lanes of a shopping arcade. In contrast to Asakusa, it is in fact still the custom in the nearby Fukagawa district for the *mikoshi* bearers to use the cry *'wasshoi!'*

Part IV

Missoku and Japanese Culture

Chapter 7

A Culture of Calmness

Korea is often described using the epithet 'the land of morning calm'; 'morning calm' being a literal translation of the two Chinese characters traditionally used as the name of the country. But considering the characteristics of Japanese culture, I wonder if it is not Japan that deserves to be thought of as 'the land of calm'.

We are all aware of the richness and distinctiveness of Japanese culture. While incorporating aspects of the cultures of other countries, Japan's position as an island nation has meant that it developed these importations in a distinctive manner, resulting in the emergence over the centuries of a uniquely sophisticated culture of its own. Such is the generally accepted theory, but it seems to me that the method of breathing employed by Japanese people is reflected strongly in Japanese culture and needs to be taken into account in this regard.

Under the influence of Japan's distinctive natural environment and lifestyle, the Japanese people have traditionally adopted a low centre of gravity in order to obtain a physique with an extremely good sense of centring. The Missoku breathing method involves constantly tilting the pelvis and using the strength of the legs, hips and abdomen, resulting in the cultivation of a sensibility in which both the individual and their environment are seen through the prism of calmness. In a world of calm the mind is tranquil while the senses become acutely responsive, thereby enabling a sensitive, finely tuned response to the smallest change. This in turn results in an excessive emphasis on detail, with importance being placed more on secondary rather than primary structures. This is clearly a formative factor underlying Japanese culture. Let's take a look at the features of the sensibility inspired by Missoku and at how this sensibility is reflected in Japan's distinctive culture.

The Art of Invisibility as Practised by Ninja

One of the main skills practised by Ninja is that of rendering oneself unnoticed as if invisible, but there is more to this skill than simply moving quietly. This is clear if we consider conversely what happens when we try to make ourselves noticed. This isn't merely a question of speaking or deliberately making a noise. We sense the presence of a living being in the slightest bodily movement, in the sound of breathing, or in the physical wavering that accompanies the act of breathing.

Many Japanese when walking through city streets will have had the experience of sensing a strong physical presence close to them and then noticing that this was being generated by someone who isn't Japanese. Eye contact, manner of speaking and physical movement tends to be more insistent than is general among Japanese people. It seems to me that this is related to differences in breathing.

It isn't possible to render oneself unnoticed simply by being thoroughly quiet. The first requirement is to lower the pelvis and prevent any wavering by uniting the torso above the hips with the hips themselves. Next, by practising Missoku with extremely long exhalations, the sound of breathing and movement of air caused by breathing are brought to a stop. Then, by expanding the body from the lower abdomen up to the chest, the physical movement involved in breathing is inhibited to the maximum extent, with extensive use being made of the deep muscles. Japanese people in the past for whom the Missoku technique came quite naturally were thus able to suppress the energy and power emitted by the living organism by consciously bringing physical movement to a halt, and this is what rendering oneself invisible is all about.

The Artistry of the Kabuki and Bunraku Theatres

The heads of the male puppets that appear in the *Bunraku* theatre weigh more than eight kilograms. The National Treasure, Tamao Yoshida, would hold up this puppet head continuously in a performance lasting for one or two hours. During those parts of a play with no recitation, the puppeteer doesn't leave the stage but stays on the sidelines, during which time the puppet remains totally motionless. There's no sense that the puppeteer is even breathing. Yoshida demonstrated his total mastery of this art until his death at the age of 87 in 2006.

The Kabuki actor, Onoe Shōroku IV, was another performer with an overwhelming stage presence, although this had nothing to do with his physical size or alacrity of movement. His presence centred on his unrivalled ability to manipulate time and space at will, as typified by the Japanese aesthetic concept of Ma.

I had the opportunity to talk to him on one occasion, and I recall him discussing how conscious he was of breathing. He was raised from infancy watching his father practise his roles in his studio. He said that it was most probably then that he learned how to exhale while maintaining the position of the abdomen. Masters of the traditional performing arts have always been fully aware that posture, movement and the type of breathing that underpins them can only be grasped on the physical level. The everyday custom of wearing a kimono with an obi sash tied above the pelvis has also been a major factor in supporting the bodies of the Japanese people. A certain dancer remarked about the Kabuki actor, Nakamura Utaemon, that it seemed as if a pole with a freely elastic pointing arrow attached to it were attached to his coccyx, enabling him to find the ideal position for his centre of gravity on the stage and to dance through the air on top of it.

Westerners tend to walk by transferring the centre of gravity from the right foot to the hips and then from the hips to the left foot as they advance. But if one walks with the pelvis tilted, the centre of gravity is constantly located somewhere below the pelvis or the coccyx. A feature of this posture is the lack of movement of the centre of gravity. This is the posture assumed by humanoid robots, probably because it's easier to get a robot to walk with minimal movement of the centre of gravity. The whole body needs to move in order to maintain balance when the centre of gravity is moved. But if the centre of gravity remains steady, it's possible to move the body merely with movement of the legs. In other words, all parts other than the pelvis and the one leg supporting the pelvis can be moved independently and freely, thereby permitting movement independent of gravitation. This in turn makes it possible to move around creating the effect of floating in mid-air.

A comparison between the dance style of the Noh theatre and Western dance is also instructive in this regard. Jumping provides a particularly noticeable difference. In the case of a dynamic dance style, dancers have to remove the centre of gravity away from their legs in order to convey a sense of flight, for example by leaping up high or by rotating. In the Noh theatre, however, the dancers do not leap up. They are able to convey a sense of flight as if floating in mid-air merely by raising their feet slightly. This shows how perceptions vary in accordance with the shared awareness of stillness possessed by performers and audience.

The Secrets of the Arts of Calligraphy and Scent

In his book *Kokyū nyūmon* (An Introduction to Breathing), Takashi Saitō describes the relationship between handling of the calligraphy brush and breathing in the following terms:

'Calligraphy is the art of breathing. The relationship between how the brush is handled and breathing appear directly in the script. If you breathe in at the moment when you have to draw a completely straight line in one breath, the flow will be broken and it will be impossible to create a flowing line. You hold your breath at the point where the brush stops. Similarly, when you make an upward brush stroke, you exhale the air stored in your lungs, and when you then raise the pen from the paper, you relax your breath as you exhale.' (Saitō, 2003, p.39.)

Japanese calligraphy had already developed into a sophisticated art form by the time the hiragana script became diffused during the Heian Period. In an article entitled *Hiragana no nazo o toku* (Solving the Riddle of Hiragana), the celebrated calligrapher, Kyūyō Ishikawa, stated as follows in connection with a poem from the early Heian Period imperial anthology *Kokin wakashū*, written by calligraphers on a folding screen (*byōbū*) and a sliding screen (*fusuma*):

'In Japan there has been a sense of interchange between painting and poetry, with calligraphy as presented in books and on *shikishi* cards constantly veering in the direction of painting. Poetry and calligraphy are arts that develop in a linear fashion within time but are translated into the form of spatial art through the separation of characters in such a way as to obscure the linguistic meaning. The spatial structure of the characters denoting "autumn wind" evokes the composition of celebrated paintings on folding screens.' (Ishikawa, 2006, p.43.)

The pleasure gained from reading a poem, copying it as calligraphy and then elucidating it thus interacts with other art forms, resulting in further transformation and re-elucidation through an astonishing sharing of sensibility.

Something similar can be seen in the art of scent, which began during the Heian Period as a sophisticated diversion involving comparison of different types of incense (*takimono-awase*). Under the name *Kōdō*, this art flourished among the samurai class during the Muromachi Period. The formal setting of Kōdō closely resembles that of the tea ceremony (*Sadō*). Those taking part sample (the Japanese verb *kiku* employed in this context actually means 'listen to') a scent and have to guess what it is. In the style of the art of scent known as *kumikō*, a theme is taken from a classical poem, on the basis of which several different types of incense are burnt. With this theme retained in their minds, the participants have to differentiate between the scents. This is not merely a question of guesswork. As in the case of the tea ceremony and calligraphy, the participants give vent to their imagination, interpreting a sensual stimulus in terms of fusion with other art forms, engaging in a synaesthetic play of the imagination in the realm of sensory stimulation.

Japan is surely the only country where scent fulfils more than a subsidiary role and where it plays a leading role to which the other arts are subsidiary. The sense of smell tends to be the least acute of all the five senses, and it was no doubt because of this that the art of scent was taken up by the samurai class as a vehicle for the pursuit of mental concentration.

The Tastes of Japanese Cuisine

It's too simplistic to ascribe the high quality of Japanese cuisine solely to the rich supply of seasonal ingredients and the outstanding skills of Japanese chefs. People in every country make efforts to eat the tastiest local food materials.

It's clear though that Japan's immediate neighbours in China and Korea have a preference for much stronger flavours and scents than those predominant in Japan. I'm not the type of person who finds any cuisine other than Japanese unpalatable, but I must admit that when I come home to Japan after an extended period overseas, the first thing I want to eat is something as simple and bland as *ochazuke*, rice soaked in tea. In the case of Chinese cuisine, I simply can't cope with the real thing as prepared by native chefs and tend to opt instead for restaurants where the chefs are Japanese. Strong flavours are just too much to cope with when I'm feeling exhausted.

Such a reaction is the consequence of a long culture in which Missoku has led to greater and greater sensitivity of sensual perception. We're able to detect the most minute variation in tastes involving acidity, saltiness, oiliness, *umami*, fragrance and sensation on the palate. Chefs from other countries have recently begun to attempt to explain the Japanese concept of umami. Since eating is a basic requirement and pleasure, such sensations need to be valued. This is why Japanese cuisine regards factors such as visual appearance and mood as so important. The following passage appears in Natsume Sōseki's novel *Kusamakura*:

'Japanese cuisine, be it in the form of soup, confectionery or sashimi, is beautifully prepared. Sitting in front of a *kaiseki* layout of dishes, it would seem to have been worthwhile visiting the restaurant for the sheer visual pleasure even if one had not so much as touched the food with one's chopsticks.' (Natsume, 2002, p.49.)

Which implies that one can experience a wonderful meal simply by looking at it!

The Philosophy of Architecture

In his book *Interia to Nihonjin* (Interior Design and the Japanese), the designer, Shigeru Uchida, states that the main feature of Japanese spatial design lies in what he describes as 'the sense of the horizontal'. He writes as follows:

'The horizontal lines of the eaves [of the Katsura Rikyū Detached Palace in Kyoto], the small walls set in the space up to the narrow *kamoi* boards set at the top of the room, the *shōji* screens set between the upper *kamoi* boards and the *shikii* doorsill, and the horizontal orientation of the raised floors present an exclusively horizontal aspect.' (Uchida, 2000, p.94.)

The inside and the outside of the building are identical as regards this emphasis on the horizontal plane. In contrast, Western style architecture is essentially vertical in orientation, with the windows generally higher than they are wide. Uchida analyses this in terms of the differing perspectives and approaches resulting from a sedentary culture and a standing culture, although this feature of Western architecture also appears to reflect the use of abdominal breathing as a physical characteristic of Westerners.

In the case of up and down movement, the vertical axis may seem beautiful, but any sense of linear, horizontal beauty is absent. But with a lowered, firmly set pelvis, tranquil breathing and lack of bodily movement, the beauty of horizontal line comes into vivid relief. Herein lies the beauty generated by the staggered shelves (*chigaidana*) that are often incorporated into the *tokonoma* alcoves of Japanese style rooms.

Such considerations bring to mind the movies of the great Japanese director, Yasujirō Ozu. The viewer's eyes don't move up and down the screen in Ozu's films. The composition of every scene always has a horizontal orientation with no vertical movement on the part of the actors, whose faces remain constantly at the same height with a subtly lowered line of vision. In order to emphasise the horizontal lines, the camera is always set in a low position, since the composition would appear flat if the camera were set above. Ozu's cameraman, Yūharu Atsuta, apparently used to crawl around on his hands and knees as he filmed. This was how he succeeded in ensuring that features of traditional architecture such as the outdoor veranda (*engawa*), tatami matting, low dining tables (*chabudai*) and *kamoi* boards are conveyed with a sense of linearity rather than as merely flat, lifeless objects.

Ozu's movies have none of the thrills and excitement of the films of Akira Kurosawa, but nevertheless enjoy widespread popularity, and not simply among film buffs. One of the reasons for their initial popularity seems to me to have been that many early viewers of Ozu's movies still retained the traditional physical characteristics associated with the Japanese people. No modern innovations are incorporated into how the film's story develops or how the actors deliver their lines, but minimal changes are effectively conveyed within a tranquil framework of space and time. The reason that Ozu's films remain as popular as ever is that contemporary viewers feel drawn into the tempo of the films and by doing so in an instant regain the physical characteristics possessed by their forebears. This sensation evokes an impression otherwise hard to obtain.

In general, the absence of activity on the part of a living organism is in proportion to its sense of stillness. When asleep or physically weak, our breath becomes still and we cease to move. However, in the case of Missoku, our consciousness is awakened by taking in deep breaths while employing our posture to restrict physical movement.

In his book *Uzumoreta Nihon* (Buried Japan) Tetsurō Watsuji had the following to say about this:

'The period between December, when the final autumn leaves fall from the trees, and the end of March, when new buds begin to sprout, is one when the hills and mountains in the vicinity of Kyoto fall silent. When one looks at the movement of colour that occurs constantly between the appearance of new leaves in spring and the falling of the very same leaves in the autumn, this sense of tranquillity conveys an indescribable sense of ease and well-being.' (Watsuji, 1980, p.30.)

The stillness of mountains and the movement of colour were sensations obtained by virtue of one's body being still. By 'movement of colour' Watsuji was referring to the blossoming of trees accompanying the changing of the seasons, the darkening colour of the leaves, and their colouring with the arrival of autumn, while the 'stillness of mountains' refers to the mountain scenery during nature's winter hibernation. Although Watsuji was a philosopher, his philosophical musings were combined with an acute sense of physical sensation.

Zen and Breathing

Breathing is considered extremely important in Zen. There are many words, such as *susoku* and *kansoku*, employed in Zen to discuss methods of breathing. The komusō itinerant monks who were the main purveyors of the tradition of shakuhachi performance during the Edo Period belonged to the Fuke sect of Zen. Instead of engaging in recitation of the Buddhist sutras and Zen meditation, they employed the shakuhachi as their specific means of spiritual training.

There are two principal benefits to be gained from breathing in Zen. The first is the ability to maintain the brain and the body in optimum condition, and the second is the ability to reveal and see the world as it is. In his book *Zen to wa nani ka* (What is Zen?), D.T. Suzuki writes as follows:

'When we talk about the ume tree, we assume we know what we're referring to. It's a plant that blooms as if to herald the arrival of spring, generates fragrant blossoms, produces fruit in early summer, the fruit having a sour taste and being used for food by pickling in salt or for medicinal purposes. But however many of these attributes are combined, the end product is never going to become an ume tree … The essential features of the ume are present in what we are unable to see, and we must begin by attempting to ascertain these features.' (Suzuki, 1991, p.90–91.)

We will never get at the essence of anything however much we play around with words. Rather than relying on our readings of the sutras, it is through the actual practice of Zen that we are able to make spiritual progress. Representations in the form of the written word inevitably convey information about primary structures. Not relying on the written word means not merely seeing superficial primary structures but instead gaining a grasp of the whole, seen as a combination of primary and secondary structures.

The composer John Cage was a student of D.T. Suzuki, and in 1952 'composed' a work entitled 4'33", the first performance of which is described by Kuniharu Akiyama in his book *Gendai ongaku o dō kiku ka* (How to Listen to Contemporary Music):

'The pianist David Tudor appeared on the stage and bowed to the audience. He then sat in front of the piano. But all he did then was to stare intently at the score on the stand in front of him and made no attempt to actually play. Despite the work supposedly consisting of three movements, at no moment did he produce a sound on the instrument. Once four minutes and thirty-three seconds had passed, the pianist closed the score, quietly stood up, bowed again to the audience and left the stage ... John Cage commented later about this performance that "while the first movement was under way, all the audience could hear was the sound of the wind blowing through the trees outside the hall. The second movement featured the sound of raindrops pattering on the roof, while the third movement was supplemented by the sound of the audience getting restless".' (Akiyama, 1973, p.17–18.)

What Cage was attempting to do was to show that secondary structures also constitute music by uncompromisingly doing away with the primary structure. An extensive debate has taken place on 4′33″ during the period of more than half a century since it was conceived with the effect of changing the course of Western musical history. But, in a sense, there is nothing particularly shocking about the conceptual basis of this piece for Japanese people, who regularly place importance on secondary structures. For example, at the end of a concert of traditional Japanese music it's by no means unusual for a member of the audience to praise the exquisite blend between the music and the sound of the wind outside the hall or the wonderful way in which the shakuhachi was able to dialogue with the twittering of birds. What are considered to be major historical events in a Western context lurk within the everyday sensory apparatus of Japanese people. This is because Zen and the breathing that forms the backbone of Zen practice have been absorbed into Japanese people's daily lives.

Breathing deeply and slowly has many beneficial effects for our body and mind. We are able to concentrate with our brain in a relaxed state and, just like a gyroscope, our brain can function at a rapid speed while our body remains still. By virtue of remaining calm, the world appears in clear resolution, including both primary and secondary structures.

One of the aims of Zen is to ascertain the truth of the world from within this mental state. Put differently, breathing makes it possible to control the relationship between oneself and the external world.

Chapter 8

Focusing In and Out

The astonishing sense of calm resulting from the combination of Japanese posture with Missoku has given rise to an even more mysterious range of sensation. While breathing normally, try focusing on a single point far away. It will initially appear out of focus, but your eyes will soon adapt to bring it into focus. But then look at a point some distance away after concentrating on Missoku breathing for five minutes or so. You'll find that you can focus immediately on the point from a wide angle of vision.

Think of a hand-held camera and a camera fixed on a tripod. In both cases the camera has an autofocus function and the camera on the tripod will be able to focus instantaneously irrespective of distance. However, in the case of the handheld camera, focusing will take some time, proportionate to the extent that your hand is moving. Similarly, time will be needed to focus if your body is moving as a consequence of keeping the pelvis upright and practising abdominal or chest breathing, whereas the stable posture that results from tilting the pelvis, combined with the stillness acquired through Missoku, makes it possible to focus in and out in an instant, as if no time had passed at all. Let's take a look at how this sensation has influenced Japanese culture.

Kimono Patterns

A foreign friend once told me that she thought that the way that Japanese people coordinate their clothing is taken to extremes. Perhaps the most typical example of such excess is the *komon* style of kimono that used to be worn by elderly Japanese women. My friend was raised in Boston, one of America's most sophisticated cities, and from having lived in Boston myself I recall that most people used to wear clothing coordinated in just one or two colours. She thought that, on the whole, Japanese tended to be excessive and lacking in a sense of fashion, but I found it impossible to concur with this judgment.

Early in spring, women might wear kimono with a detailed flower basket pattern together with a woven obi with a butterfly pattern. The obi support might have an *ume* pattern, while the *haori* cloak might incorporate a vertical or horizontal striped pattern. This is a brilliant and vivid reflection of the seasons. What we're doing in this case is not seeing the woman as a totality so much as focusing on a particular feature of the kimono to enjoy the design or focusing on the neckband in order to admire the borders between the *komon* patterns on the cloak and the kimono. We can thus take in and enjoy various different features instantaneously at the same time.

These *komon* patterns can be viewed to some extent from a wide perspective so as to reveal the beauty of several dozen combinations of patterns, or we can focus in on a single pattern to the exclusion of all else. There are various ways in which kimono can be admired; the patterns appearing on kimono are employed deliberately in order to explore the various possibilities available. This is an essential feature of the Japanese kimono.

It's possible that the Japanese style of coordination is incompatible with the essential features of Western style clothing, but the Japanese style is rooted in the Japanese aesthetic and is therefore based on different criteria.

The Meaning of *Iki*

In his book *Iki no kōzō* (The Structure of Iki), Shūzō Kuki describes coquettishness (along with stylishness, one of the nuances of the Japanese term *iki*) as a subtle suggestion directed toward the opposite sex. In other words, it is described as something that should not be directly revealed but be merely hinted at. Such an indirect approach has the effect of emphasising the mood of seductiveness.

This idea is at the opposite pole from the Western idea of coquettishness and seductiveness. In the West, the sexy actress is typified by figures such as Rita Heyworth and Marilyn Monroe, who leave nothing to the imagination. Such actresses convey an overwhelming sense of health and attractiveness, but this is far from the way in which Japanese people have traditionally viewed the sense of seductiveness.

The Western approach is easy to appreciate if one adopts a total viewpoint. But a Japanese woman's seductiveness may be revealed in her eyes, the nape of her neck, the pattern of her kimono, or the occasional glimpse of her ankle. The point of focus is constantly changing and there is no total, overall sense of seductiveness as in the West. Rather than revealing seductiveness as a whole, the totality is deliberately hidden and seductiveness becomes evident in tiny details, thereby emphasising its impact. The sensibility and ability to appreciate such details is the prerequisite in this regard. It's generally assumed that Japanese people today have become far removed from such a subtle sensibility, but is this really the case?

Time and Space in Gardens

On a visit to a large garden in England I once walked along a path and first encountered a long hedge on both sides. This was followed by flowerbeds with a profusion of red flowers, beyond which there was a luxurious rose garden opposite a pond full of water lilies and then a garden of daffodils. My experience of this garden was like a narrative taking shape along a time axis. Each vista presented simple colours and forms. For example, the hedge consisted entirely of the same plants, all of the same height and the same colour. The overall structure of the garden had clearly been rigorously planned. In contrast, Japanese gardens are generally appreciated from a seated position inside the room that overlooks them. Gardens such as those of the Ryōanji temple and the Kokedera garden at the Saihōji temple in Kyoto are hard to appreciate when viewed from a Western perspective.

In connection with the garden of the Tōfukuji temple, Roland Barthes wrote the following passage in his book on Japanese aesthetics entitled *Hyōchō no teikoku* (Empire of Signs):

'There are no flowers and no footprints. Where are the human beings? They are present in the carrying of the rocks, in the sweeping of the broom, in other words in the workings of the expressed object.' (Barthes, 1974, p.104.)

Barthes was clearly aware of how this garden served as a tool for focusing in and out. While looking at the garden, at one moment one's eyes may move in the direction of the water plants in a pond, whereas at the next moment one observes the whole expanse of the garden. At one moment one may be looking at a falling autumnal leaf and at another moment at the autumn leaves and the view of the moss. The strokes of the broom over the gravel may create the impression of a stream of water, meaning that one sometimes sees something that is actually not there at all. Since the viewer is constantly applying a varied focus, the garden seems to represent the whole of creation as a microcosm of the universe. There is no main structure, and human agency is recognisable solely in the subsidiary structures.

In the case of an English garden, a tale seems to unfold as one walks through it. In contrast, in a Japanese garden the viewer creates his own sense of three-dimensionality on a superficially flat plane, giving rise to time. This process results in an interchange between time and space.

Blank Space in Paintings

Upon seeing a painting entitled *Nachi Waterfall* dating from the Kamakura Period, André Malraux remarked that he had never seen a painting of such depth before. For me as an amateur in this field, Japanese paintings in the *Nihonga* style seem almost two-dimensional in their absence of perspective.

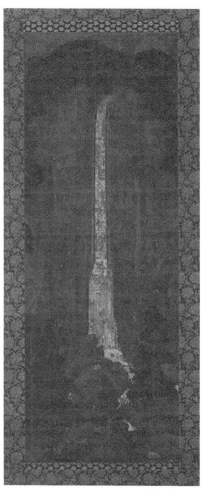

National Treasure 'Nachi Waterfall'. Hanging scroll; ink and colour on silk. Height: 160.3cm; Width: 58.5cm. Kamakura Period; 13th –14th Century. (Nezu Museum)

I think this can be explained in the following way. For example, no matter how deep a space created through application of perspective may be, the fact that this space is prescribed by perspective means that it is finite. However, the space present within a picture with no such artificial prescriptions that emerges as a consequence of focusing in is essentially infinite.

Experts in this field may be able to explain why Japanese artists didn't develop perspective or didn't even become aware of it, but it seems to me that the reason lies in the way that Japanese people view things. Perspective involves representing things that are close by making them relatively larger than those far away, and thus establishing a sense of primary and secondary qualities within a painting. But being able to focus in and out and therefore not needing to posit primary and secondary qualities results in an increase in freedom. Take the example of the famous work *Kakitsubata-zu* (Irises) by Ogata Kōrin. A vast number of irises are depicted on the left side of a folding screen, but there is no real centre. This might be contrasted with Picasso's *Two Women Running on the Beach*. A comparison of these two paintings shows that they are so different as to make one wonder whether they are products of the same art form.

The women painted by Picasso possess radiant skin and anyone who sees this painting is likely to gain an impression of vitality, dynamism and beauty. Picasso is striving here to express himself with the utmost clarity. In contrast, Japanese paintings prior to the introduction of Western artistic techniques assumes a meaning on a different dimension from painting that incorporates a strong expressive emphasis of its own. Ogata Kōrin's *Kakitsubata-zu* is certainly beautiful, but it was not painted in order to emphasise its beauty. One gains the impression that the spatial configuration, underpinned as it is by a stylised form of beauty, is intended to provide a place for reflection. The painting itself does not attempt to tell a story of

some kind. Rather, it might be likened to a vessel that opens the
way to free reflection on the part of the viewer.

National Treasure 'Irises' by Ogata Kōrin. Right screen of pair;
6 panels; ink and colour on gold-foiled paper. Height: 151.2cm;
Width: 358.8cm. Edo Period; 18th Century. (Nezu Museum)

Picasso, *Two Women Running on the Beach* (1922), as it appears
at the top on the front cover of Volume IV of *Pikaso zenshū*.
(Complete works of Picasso)

It is common in Japanese gardens and paintings for the main subjects to be placed at the edge or in an unimposing position so as to encourage the viewer to focus in and out. In his book *Miru kiku yomu* (Look, Listen, Read), Claude Lévi-Strauss wrote as follows about Hokusai's *Hundred Views of Mount Fuji*:

'Just as Proust worked with scraps of paper, the pictures of Mount Fuji suggest that what Hokusai did was to gather together in disregard of scale the details and fragments of landscapes that he had drawn on the basis of personal observation in his sketchbooks and then compose the pictures on this basis.' (Lévi-Strauss, 2005, p.6.)

There is no primary and secondary ranking of subject matter here. Perspective is essentially a question of the ranking of subject matter in order to determine the spatial composition. In Japanese pictorial composition the parts and the whole are constantly in opposition. There is no sense of one particular element being more important than any other within the whole, which presents a flat surface that enables the viewer to focus on any of the parts.

In the book *Super Flat*, the contemporary artist, Takashi Murakami, defines Japanese culture as 'super flat'. He dissects Tokyo stations to set them out on a plane surface and analyses the paintings of artists such as Itō Jakuchū and animation.

Thoroughly dismantling and splitting up the hierarchical ranking of space as carried out through the application, modern computer graphics technology provides a fine example of what I mean by focusing in. The perfection of detail gives rise to 'white space'. I feel this represents an attempt to extend the sensation that emerges from Missoku into the modern era.

Kuroko and Manga

There are four puppeteers assigned to each puppet in the Bunraku theatre: the lead puppeteer (*kashira*), the puppeteer who operates the puppet's right hand (*omozukai*) and two assistants (*kuroko*). The *omozukai* plays the leading role, while the *kuroko* wear black costumes intended to create the illusion that they are invisible, despite their being plainly visible. The audience accepts this convention and affects not to see them. They in no way detract from the audience's capacity to be profoundly moved by the narrative in which the puppets are the players. Indeed, in the past some spectators were so emotionally affected that they were led to commit suicide after having attended a Bunraku puppet play on the theme of a love suicide. Audiences today are free to transfer their attention to any one of the constitutive elements of the genre: the puppets, the *omozukai* puppeteer, the *kuroko* and the *jōruri* narrator. We are engaged in focusing in and out between fiction and reality.

A similar feature can be observed in modern *manga*, in which a handwritten monologue may suddenly appear independently of the lines of the main characters and the use of onomatopoeia with the intention of avoiding monotony through the incorporation of a secondary structure containing clarification of nuance or humorous asides.

A comparison between the American comic *Batman* and the Japanese comic *Dragonball* is revealing in this regard. There is very little movement in *Batman*, which moves forward solely on the basis of the strength of the images. However real the depiction may be, the images never leave the realm of the two-dimensional. On the other hand, *Dragonball* gives the impression of moving forward together with the sensibility of the reader. We notice the movement of someone else when we come to a stop. It is this stopping that causes the manga to move. Japanese manga and animation have gained a worldwide reputation, ascribable to the extraordinary degree of freedom of interpretation that results from an emphasis on detail and secondary structure.

Haiku, the Tea Ceremony, Ajikan

The *haiku* is the briefest verse form in any of the world's major literatures. What's more, it incorporates various prescriptions such as a requirement to include seasonal words. How did it come about that such a verse form should have emerged in Japan? One of the most well-known haiku is that by Matsuo Bashō: *Furuike ya / Kawazu tobikomu / Mizu no oto* (An old pond / A frog jumps in / The sound of water). The original idea for this haiku was suggested by Bashō's pupil, Kikaku, who proposed the opening line *Yamabuki ya*, after the name of the Japanese rose plant. The verse leaves itself open to a variety of interpretations and cannot be considered descriptive. Readers are free to conjure up their own image of the pond and of how the frog jumps into it, or they can imagine themselves as the frog. One could equally imagine a scene in the middle of the night when the only perception available is the sound.

When we hear the word *hana*, meaning flowers or blossoms and often referring specifically to cherry blossoms, we conjure up the image of spring scenery, of the various temporal springs that we have experienced in the past, and the various expressions of spring that we have encountered indirectly in stories, paintings and other haiku. We're able to superimpose a variety of different images, thereby bringing about a vast accumulation of images. By virtue of being so brief, the haiku enables us to focus in and out on many dimensions. Minimising the number of words and syllables gives free scope to the imagination, thereby opening up an infinite range of expressive potential.

The combination of 5-7-5 syllables and the convention regarding the use of seasonal terms imposes restrictions that are similarly intended to give free rein to the imagination.

When we enter the enclosed space of a tatami-matted room of the type used in the tea ceremony, the small size of the room is likely to induce a sense of claustrophobia in many of us today. Once the ceremony gets under way we can no longer engage in small talk and thus become conscious of our breathing and the rustling of our clothing in the tranquil atmosphere, forcing us to retreat into ourselves. We then enter a state of quiet ecstasy as we experience a variety of sensual stimuli: the crackling of the charcoal on the brazier, the bubbling of the boiling water, the scent of incense, and the calligraphy on the scroll hanging in the darkly lit tokonoma alcove. As we sip the slowly prepared tea, a mere two or three sips of the bitter liquid seem to pervade our whole being.

Isolation from the outside world and from information is said to encourage the appearance of illusions and hallucinations. Restricting external stimulation increases the proportion of images that arise inside the brain. Our perception of real time and space gets distorted and a separate world emerges in which various elements are blended. Zen meditation has a similar effect, but the tea ceremony provides the ideal setting for this approach.

Over the years the room in which the tea ceremony is held has increasingly done away with decoration and has become gradually smaller. The miniaturisation of the room by Sen no Rikyū, the founder of the tea ceremony as we know it today, occurred in order to enable this microcosmos, with its flowers, vases, tea ceremony implements, and minimal use of words and gestures, to encourage a leap of perception and awareness into one's own microcosmos and finally into one's own brain.

The word *ajikan* is defined as follows in one of Japan's most authoritative dictionaries, the Kōjien, as 'A method of contemplating the truth of non-life in esoteric Buddhism by representing the letter "A" as the origin of all things.' (Shinmura, 1976, p.34.)

This is a form of spiritual training employed in esoteric Buddhism based on the belief that the first letter of the Sanskrit alphabet subsumes all of creation. It involves imagining the character in one's head so as to distance oneself from it or bring it up closer. It entails a moving of focus whereby the letter 'A' is taken to the far ends of the universe to be viewed as a tiny object which is then expanded to become an entity far larger than oneself.

The next stage involves uniting oneself with the object. This is the first time that the object of meditation is introduced into the brain, entailing a mental movement of focus. Expansion and contraction occur inside the brain, resulting in an awareness of active and passive inclusion and of unity. This is a sensation that has much in common with the way in which we can appreciate haiku and the tea ceremony.

As a consequence of the sense of calm that results from Missoku and the perspective obtained by focusing in and out, our bodies become sensitive to and are stimulated by a variety of parameters such as timing, speed, temperature, aural dynamics and pitch, space, touch, and smell. These parameters then lose their individual identities, coming together to constitute a single entity. This interaction between the parameters and their coming together is a phenomenon that arises within the brain. The sensation brought about through normal breathing in the Missoku manner is very close to the ultimate goal sought after in esoteric Buddhism.

Chapter 9

The Concept of Ma

Definition of Ma

Ma is a distinctively Japanese concept. Although one of the basic concepts in Japanese aesthetics, the word is used frequently in colloquial expressions such as *ma ni au* ('to be in time') and *ma ga warui* ('ill-timed' or 'embarrassing'). Let's take a look at what the word really means.

I often end workshops in the conventional Japanese manner with a collective single clap following an introductory call (*iyo~*). When I try to get Westerners to do this, they rarely manage to synchronise their clap and the only way they succeed in doing so is if I add a count, 'one, two, three ...'. With no such marker to rely on, they find such synchronisation difficult. But if I try the same thing with a Japanese audience, even one consisting of a couple of thousand people, they manage to come together in perfect synchronisation with the clap. This applies no matter the register, timbre or volume of the introductory call.

It's clear that Westerners hear and feel something different from the Japanese and it seems to me that this difference arises due to the difference between Missoku breathing and other methods of breathing.

Ma is essentially a question of timing on the temporal level and of balance of layout on the spatial level. In both the temporal and spatial contexts, it remains no matter what attempts are made to disrupt it. Changes in register, timbre or volume that may have the effect of expanding or shrinking time in an absolute sense have no effect on *Ma*, which remains intact regardless.

It's only natural that Westerners should think of time as an absolute, independent entity, whereas Japanese think of it as something that can get warped through the effect of other elements. To be more specific, although the time axis and three-dimensional space are determined physically, once other elements come into play, such as sound and vibration, light and colour, and smell, or the expression on a person's face or one's relationship with another person, the sensual perceptions of the recipient become warped.

When we experience drastic changes in our immediate environment, for example in forms such as thunder and lightning, typhoons and earthquakes, we may feel that a specific duration has passed in an instant or that it has lasted an eternity. The roar of nature may weigh heavily on us and make us aware of our own insignificance in the scheme of things. We may be driving along an expressway at over a hundred miles an hour, but it may seem that we are virtually stationary. Conversely, we may be standing still in the middle of a storm, but we may have the sensation that we are actually moving.

When confronted by such manifestations of out-of-the-ordinary energy we frequently experience the disappearance of the borders that set the limits of time, space, light and sound, which seem to mix, to blend together or to become warped. But if our bodies remain calm due to our practice of Missoku, we become sensitive to the smallest change. Our sensations, unrestricted by the physical boundaries of time and space, expand as a consequence of focusing in and out and of the effects of harmonics.

The various factors that we experience in the course of everyday life result in the warping of our experience of time and space. We sense a tranquil storm within the passage of everyday life. This is the sensation of Ma. The culture of Ma comes into being when we interpret such subtle elements and these elements interplay.

Facing Off in Martial Arts

The essential difference between a Japanese martial art such as kendo and its Western equivalent, fencing, is evident in the movements involved. Fencing requires a preparatory movement from which to act along with absolute rapidity of motion.

In contrast, there is no such movement in the traditional art of Japanese swordsmanship. Relative speed is required, with the key to victory being the ability to confuse the opponent by making them misjudge one's timing. Missoku makes it possible to reduce to an absolute minimum the amount of time it takes to inhale, thereby expanding the range of possibilities for selecting the moment when one gets into action. By restricting one's breathing so that an opponent is unaware of it and by doing away with the need for any preparatory movement, it's also possible to confuse one's opponent by giving them no hint as to the moment when the next attack is going to take place.

Staying still has the effect of stopping the transmission of any information about one's physical movement and concealing the *primary structure,* that is to say the instant of attack. Kendo is a contest in which the opponents attempt to interpret each other's breathing and destroy their sense of timing and balance, that is to say Ma.

A similar feature can be observed in the traditional board games of *Go* and *Shōgi*. Yoshiharu Hanyū, one of Japan's leading Shōgi players, has written about how, when he's up against an opponent in top form, he rises above himself. In the morning when he enters the room where the match is to take place and he exchanges greetings with his opponent, he can tell exactly what state the other person is in. He writes that Japanese people used to have the ability to instantaneously read another person's state of mind with their own mind's eye. This is an aspect of all forms of combat unique to the Japanese people, who have developed the ability to acquire information on the level of subsidiary structure.

The Imaginative Space of Rakugo

Rakugo, the traditional Japanese art of storytelling, is another art for which Ma is of the essence. There is here no explanation, no overt expression, no psychological portrayal in words.

In the case of Western storytelling and monodramas, intricate depiction of emotion and emotional expression tend to be indispensable features. But in the case of Rakugo, a single call of a person's name is able to convey distance, location and situation, with the listeners gaining the impression that they have entered directly into the conversation. A simple gesture, facial expression, movement of the eyes and nuance of intonation reveals the whole of a space and environment distanced from the real world. The Rakugo narrator is in a sense engaged in a performance that involves tricking their audience.

The story is carefully elaborated, but prime importance is placed on how it is told. The subsidiary structure takes the place of the primary structure. This is an environment dominated by *Ma*, and audiences take pleasure in the art by assimilating themselves into it. In this sense the famous Rakugo artist, Shijaku Katsura, was an artist of a modern, Western type who would carefully analyse the primary structure and reconstitute it in order to demonstrate new horizons. He deserves the greatest respect for this. But conversely, this results in a diminution of the effectiveness of the subsidiary structure. In addition, he would sit with a raised pelvis and breathe through the mouth, thus making it difficult to give rise to a consummate sense of Ma.

In contrast, another celebrated Rakugo artist, Danshi Tatekawa, may not have made as much effort as Shijaku Katsura in putting together the primary structure, but he had an outstanding ability to assimilate with the situation. He kept his pelvis low and exhibited a wonderful sense of Ma. I imagine he practised the Missoku method of breathing, and it was this that resulted in his intuitive capacity to portray an imaginative space before his audience.

Spoken Dialogue in the Films of Yasujirō Ozu

The dialogue in the films of Yasujirō Ozu is highly distinctive. The sensitive lines delivered by the actors in the most matter of fact manner may not be a faithful representation of everyday speech at the time, but they nevertheless succeed in the most brilliant manner in conveying and highlighting the ideas on which the movie is based. An international symposium was held in 2003 to mark the centenary of Ozu's birth. On that occasion, the film director, Yōichi Sai, remarked that the era in which Ozu's films were set was one when demeanour and deportment somehow held sway over human emotions; in other words demeanour was itself a mode of expression.

The fact that deportment can itself be a means of expression implies the existence of a shared sensibility and aesthetic that means that we are all able to discover something in the most subtle of variations. Yasujirō Ozu was born during the Meiji era, when it was general for artists, spectators and audiences to tilt their pelvises and practise Missoku breathing. For such people the sense of Ma was something that came completely naturally, so that the most subtle nuance was imbued with meaning. For Japanese people in an era now passed, Ma was a standard part of the Japanese language.

Today there are TV commercials and dramas employing dialogue that seems to parody Ozu's most famous film, *Tokyo Story*. They fail and come across as trite and clichéd because the demeanour and deportment of the actors in Ozu's work is totally absent from them. This isn't simply because of the nature of the production itself. It's a result of the fact that both the performers and the listeners now practise abdominal breathing with the pelvis raised and with an unstable angle of vision, meaning that their speaking and understanding of the Japanese language is no longer mediated by the sense of Ma.

The Other Dimension of the Noh Theatre

The Noh stage presents a stylised environment from which all superfluous dramatic ornament has been totally excluded. The *hashigakari* passageway along which the characters in the drama pass as they make their way onto the stage is set at a right angle horizontally to the stage, a position which contrasts with the diagonal positioning of the *hanamichi* passageway onto the stage in the Kabuki theatre. The Noh stage is thus constructed in an essentially flat manner.

The players in the primary and secondary roles are never set in opposition to one another and never radically change their positions on the stage. The location never changes and there is no sense of three-dimensionality. This means that the audience inevitably find themselves focusing on a variety of elements on the stage. The stylised pine tree depicted at the back of the stage constitutes one of these elements. As in the case of the tea ceremony, the spatial restriction brings about a leap of consciousness within the brain. In other words, the art of Noh might be thought of as a tool that transports the consciousness into a world of imagery.

The undecorated, flat Noh stage, as in the world of the tea ceremony, brings about a fusion between inner consciousness and the external world within a rigorously delimited spatial environment. This is symbolised by the appearance of motifs from the other world, in the form of spirits and ogres.

The main theme of Noh plays tends to be the subtle point of contact between the real world and other worlds. The act of going back and forth between the real world and a world of the imagination or another dimension that exists solely within the brain is realised in the world of the Noh theatre. The Noh theatre is an art in which space is subsumed within time by means of a variety of elements including special overtones and breathing, resulting in a distortion of time and space and, in the final analysis, a comprehensive awareness of all these elements. Among the classical Japanese stage arts, Noh is an art that epitomises Ma in the sense that it deliberately confuses and distorts the parameters of sound, space, time and breath and attempts to transport the spectator into his own brain and onto another dimension. Much of interest remains to be said about the Noh theatre, but I shall leave this for a later chapter.

The Sense of *Ma*

In addition to my work as a shakuhachi soloist, I'm also the leader of the band Kokoo that includes the shakuhachi and the *koto*, and I've worked extensively on sessions with musicians both in Japan and overseas. Musicians from other countries are unable to perform intuitively with the Japanese sense of *Ma*, meaning that sessions have to be held in line with the Western sensibility with recourse to rhythm and meter. Nevertheless, the most gifted musicians do indeed manage to produce sounds at exactly the right moment in time as a reflection of Ma. Such musicians possess an outstanding sense of rhythm in the Western sense but at the same time have a very acute sensibility. They are able to respond to and empathise with subtle variations in tone colour and distortions of time that I come up with when playing and are able to perform with the same acute awareness of Ma as that possessed by the finest performers of traditional Japanese music.

This sensibility varies among Japanese people in accordance with age. The dividing line now seems to appear at around the age of 80. People above that age have acquired a sense of Ma in the most natural manner. There are differences from one person to another among people beneath that age, affected by matters such as their lifestyle and the genres of music they tend to listen to. I get the impression that there's been a slight increase in the number of traditional Japanese musicians who perform with a raised pelvis, breathe through the mouth and raise and lower their shoulders when breathing. The Ma sensibility may well be changing.

To change the subject for a moment, I heard an interesting story from a friend of mine. He's a Japanese guy who for many years has served as a musical director for overseas bands. When a problem of some kind arises, he's asked his opinion as a director. Beginning with a moment of silence intended to give added weight to his reply, he assumes that everyone will prick up their ears in anticipation of his forthcoming words of wisdom. But, contrary to expectation, everyone starts chatting away and they show no sign of waiting for his reply. In Japan, silence and a pregnant pause serve as the prelude to a forthcoming weighty remark. The longer the silence the greater the weight of the remark that follows. In the West the assumption is that the would-be speaker has nothing to say.

Despite the fact that my friend has plenty of experience of living overseas and is richly endowed musically too, he seems never to have reconciled himself on an everyday level to the inability of Westerners to interpret the meaning of breath and to realise that silence is itself a mode of verbal expression.

Part V

Harmonics — The Secret of Japanese Sound

Chapter 10

Discovering One's Own Sound World

The Enigma of Performance: Physical Properties and Rhythm

I'd like to recount another story from my period of study at the Berklee College of Music. I was in the department of composition, where classical composition is taught. But because Berklee is a college specialising in jazz, in addition to composition one has to learn an instrument in, for example, the woodwind department. The system thus involves studying jazz composition and arrangement along with instrumental performance.

The college is a very high level institution and students are presented with a mountain of work, including both composition and arrangement, to get through on a daily basis. The work is assessed and marked on a sliding scale of ten grades. This was a tough time for an impoverished foreign student who had to make ends meet by doing part time work as well. But this is a system that enables anyone minded to do so to learn. Special lessons are available to upper ranking students, meaning that the more proficient you become the more enjoyable the study experience is. In the senior ensemble class, you can form a band with brilliant performers of all kinds of instruments and I recall that this was a fantastically enjoyable experience. But there were problems I encountered that couldn't be resolved merely by means of effort and ability.

Westerners tend to have a larger lung capacity than Japanese people and their physical movements differ too due to their practice of abdominal breathing. Breathing in this way also means that when they laugh, they tend to do so in a loud and exaggerated manner that in Japan would seem overdone and something one would be likely to hear only in the theatre. These physical characteristics and this sense of rhythm are of course beneficial when one plays Western music.

I met a boy still in his teens who had just entered music college. Despite never having learned anything on a formal basis, he was able to create an incredible jazz sound and attach accents in a four-beat format in a manner that seemed way beyond my capabilities. Taking part in a jazz session, I'd produce a long tone on the shakuhachi which until then had seemed to fit into a dull and conventional rhythmic format but that had become somehow Japanese. I'd complain to my fellow musicians that my long tone was intended to provide the cue for a climax, to which they'd reply that what I was doing didn't fit with the atmosphere of jazz. But they said that they'd like to have a go at creating music in this style that they described as 'spacy' in the Japanese style. But when a saxophonist played a long tone, it seemed somehow different from what I'd been doing.

The Western posture differed from mine. They stand with their pelvis raised. You'll soon see if you deliberately try to raise your pelvis, but it becomes easy to move and, if anything, adopting a static posture becomes difficult. I knew nothing about Missoku at that time but I was aware that, in comparison with Westerners, I was tilting my pelvis. This meant that my body was relaxed. In comparison with my long tones, those produced by Westerners conveyed a sense of prescribed meter. There are times when one adds a vibrato to a note. When I do so the note seems like a straight line without any rhythmic underpinning. What was really surprising though was that the musicians I was working with immediately adapted to this new atmosphere. This troubled me and I didn't know what was going on. But since we were obliged to play jazz, I stopped producing too many long tones and felt that I had to create a sense of swing with a rhythmical feel that could be easily conveyed to my fellow musicians.

Even today it's hard to say that there's been much progress on research in connection with the relationship between bodily control during performance and breath, but at the time neither I nor the people around me knew anything about the reasons for such differences. I've also encountered the opposite phenomenon since there are plenty of things that come naturally to Japanese musicians that prove very difficult to communicate. I'd suggest, for example, that a forte should be realised with a certain degree of restraint at some particular position to which the other musicians would reply that they didn't know what I was on about. A forte is a forte. If a lower volume of sound was needed, a mezzoforte or a mezzopiano would have been written in the score. I'd point out that what I meant was not a change in dynamics but a change in tone colour.

Everyone eventually grasped what I was saying but it took a long time to convince them. It's generally assumed that Japanese and Western musicians are the same these days but when Japanese musicians perform together with Western musicians the differences soon rise to the surface.

Rhythm: Static Time versus Dynamic Time

Japanese people are by no means adept at coping with the uniform sense of rhythm prevalent in the West. In many of the world's musical cultures it's common to deliberately displace rhythm to some extent, but there are very few in which rhythm is so consistently displaced or where all the performers in an ensemble seem to come together only for them to almost immediately drift apart once again.

In the *matsuri-bayashi* ensembles that feature in traditional Japanese festivals, for example, the large drum may set out a fairly regular rhythmic pattern, but the flute player will constantly be either moving ahead of or falling back behind this rhythm. In the genre of *Jiuta*, the *shamisen* and vocal parts are fixed in the score with both parts basically consisting of the same homophonic melody, but the constant, subtle melodic and rhythmic displacement means that the listener sometimes gains the impression of the presence of a countermelody, while at other times the shamisen appears to be accompanying the singer. This clearly indicates the presence in Japan of a different conception of rhythm from that prevalent in the West.

Let's take a look at how this comes about. Traditional Japanese musicians perform with their pelvis tilted while practising Missoku breathing, meaning that there is absolutely no vertical movement of the body and no rhythm-related factors coming into play in terms of posture. Each performer demonstrates their own specific sense of rhythm resulting in the following situation arising.

Since performers of Western music practise abdominal breathing, they perform with a raised pelvis with the consequence that the slightest movement appears on the surface of the body. This is like when a group of people in a boat travel down rapids and they all share the same up and down sensation. Breathing and the body down to its deepest recesses are dominated by this sensation. Conversely, movement of the body makes the rhythm inside the brain more dynamic, a rhythm which is then amplified on the surface of the body. This makes it easy to align with the rhythm and to get into the groove. The primary structure of music may be thought of as consisting of rhythm and pitch. In the case of Japan, the subordinate structures of dynamics and timbre developed to such an extent that they eroded rhythm and pitch, as a consequence of which musical meter became flexible and changes occurred in pitch.

In the West, rhythm has a position as a primary structural element which brings about changes in the structural elements subordinate to it and sparks enjoyment among listeners. In contrast, Japanese rhythm is characterised by the transformation affected by subordinate structural elements on the primary structural elements and it's the totality of such changes that constitutes the source of enjoyment. The subordinate structures would be hard to perceive in the presence of strong gradations of rhythm as in the West. One might say that time, as experienced by people who practise abdominal breathing, might be likened to a lined notebook, in contrast to which time as experienced by those who practise Missoku breathing resembles a blank sheet of white paper.

In the case of traditional Japanese music, the rhythm internalised within individual performers is almost impossible for people in the vicinity to perceive. Each performer attempts to align their playing with that of the other members of his ensemble by listening closely to them. It's inevitable therefore that there should be a certain degree of lack of coordination between the players. If anything, listeners take pleasure in this lack of coordination, which eventually becomes fixed in such a way that the departure from the main melodic and rhythmic structures has the effect of establishing what sounds like a counter melody or an accompaniment.

Young performers of traditional Japanese music no longer share all their musical characteristics with their seniors. They were brought up listening to Western music, studied Western music in the school curriculum, and have been continuously told to practise abdominal or chest breathing in order to improve their posture. This has resulted in a posture with the pelvis raised becoming standard. One consequence of this is that the way in which they perceive rhythm has changed significantly. A strange sense of dynamism has come to dominate in performances of traditional Japanese music, with the performers incorporating expansive physical gestures and counting within a regular four-beat metrical structure. There is no such physical movement present in this music and there are times when one wonders whether the performers don't have a metronome stuck in their brains.

I vividly recall one of the last recitals given by the great koto player, Yonekawa Fumiko I, who died at the age of 92 in 2005. In her final years she found it hard to stand up and walk. She appeared on the stage accompanied by her daughter, but a totally different world opened up the moment the curtains opened. She played a very difficult fast piece but her technical mastery was just phenomenal and her stage presence was riveting. Her performance was as smooth and gliding as a hovercraft. There were no mountains and valleys and no shades of thick and thin. She remained completely immobile throughout the immaculately smooth performance. She had acquired a sense of rhythm characterised by utter smoothness with no ups and downs. I was put in mind of the martial arts expert Yoshinori Kōno's reference to use of the body without any need for preparatory movement such as twisting or bending.

People accustomed to listening to music with a groovy feel about it may perhaps find it hard to appreciate music with so little strong contrast. But any performance on such a transcendental level can surely be appreciated by listeners of all generations. Conversely, the groove that characterises African-American music, such as a jazz or soul, is a product of vibrations of the body caused by their method of breathing. With a raised pelvis, they are able to move freely from the waist above, thereby facilitating the transmission of vibrations.

My Own Music

There's no graduate school at Berklee. In order to further my studies of composition I entered the graduate school at the New England Conservatory and joined the Third Stream program. Third Stream is a musical genre that combines classical music with jazz and ethnic music. I felt that such a program had been tailor-made for me.

The course incorporated a certain amount of non-Western methodology, for example training in copying phrases produced by another musician without recourse to musical notation. It was enormously stimulating for me to come into contact with such methods. I also became aware of the almost frightening degree of depth and breadth of people in Western countries.

Take the subject of musical counterpoint for example. In Japan the student of counterpoint learns on a theoretical basis how to create a melody that can be combined with an existing melody. But in America the question of how to create a counter melody to an existing melody was subject to computer analysis based on examples extending over several centuries, with the full list compiled in a thick volume extending over several hundred pages. You'd simply have to think of a certain phrase and consult this book in the manner of a dictionary to find the right answer. The whole procedure was completely different from that followed in Japan.

Moreover, the Third Stream program encouraged students to use their ears rather than rely on musical notation and to create new music on this basis. On one particular occasion the chief professor gave a live concert with his own band. A movie was screened and they listened to the accompanying music and created new music that blended with the film music. The musicians were able to immediately work out all the keys and all the rhythms and seemed to have a superhuman ability to create music that was constantly appropriate in context. Their technical abilities were also flawless. It might not have been that interesting for those of us who were more absorbed in watching the film, but the results of their efforts were most impressive.

But it meant something else for the professor. It had no doubt taken an enormous length of time for him to train his ear and perfect his technique. I felt almost intimidated by these Westerners with their determination to systemise everything by taking things as far as they can be taken and by recording and providing evidence for everything on a scientific basis.

One experience retains a firm place in my memory. I submitted a piece I had composed to my professor at the end of the semester. Dozens of check points relating to what I'd learned in the course of the semester were then rigorously examined. He ticked me off first for using intervals that he'd told us shouldn't be used. That was one point deducted. Next, he said that my counterpoint was feeble. Another minus point. Having been through the whole piece he told me that he'd be marking me down three points. But then he told me that this means that I'd got an A grade and that I'd got the highest marks that semester. 'Fantastic! Excellent!' I asked him if he had any opinion about my piece, whether it was good or bad, whether he liked it or not. He replied by saying that he had no intention of expressing his opinion and asked me conversely how on earth it would benefit me if he were to let me know his subjective opinion. He went on as follows: 'Look, you'll be returning to Japan soon and will have to start competing on a market that I know nothing about. There's no point in me saying something about a market of which I have no knowledge and that I can only imagine. I've got a good knowledge of the American market and I'm one of its representatives but my own personal preferences do no more than reflect my own personal tastes. I've rigorously checked the extent to which you've mastered what you've been taught, and this is reflected in your results. This means that judgment on how gifted you are will differ from one market to another and from one listener to another.'

He thus refused to give his personal opinion, saying that it was outside his range of responsibility to do so. He said that this had nothing to do with the fact that the music we created was different. It was simply that he, as an individual, had no right to judge me as an individual; to do so would be meaningless and was not something that he wished to do. I was astonished that the method and system of the graduate school where I was studying and which I thought so highly of did not allow for any judgment of my work. This made me realise acutely that it is only the musician himself who is able to judge his own work.

There was a Korean guitarist I met at Berklee. Keeping up with harmony in the form of chord progressions is one of the main difficulties of jazz and much emphasis was placed on this in our studies at Berklee. However, when he played, he would maintain the same harmony for ten minutes at a time. This must have seemed tedious to any musicians who had spent their time learning how to cope with complicated chord progressions, but he was a guitarist with a great rhythmic sense whose concerts at the college were always a great success.

No matter what's taught at college, if you excel in some other field people will appreciate what you're doing and place a positive evaluation on it. I thus became strongly aware that there are no definitively correct answers in music. Rather than look for such absolutes, the important thing is to find one's own mode of expression which, if it has real value, will be positively assessed. At the same time, the college strove not just to foster individuality but also the acquisition of a vast quantity of theoretical, academic knowledge. That's why, after studying for several years in such a productive environment, I realised that I was all on my own. I finally began to become aware ever so vaguely that we are all physical manifestations of the culture and language that forms the background to the environments and ways of thinking and feeling into which we were born and raised.

Chapter 11

Japanese Tone Colour Vocal Frequency

After studying in the United States, I became aware of certain physical changes that I hadn't noticed before whenever I went back to America to work.

I attended the wedding ceremony of a friend's son in the United States. All of the groom's friends were clad in morning dress. In Japan I'd always thought of morning dress as being the ultimate in ugly clothing, but this particular group of young men looked fantastic and I realised it had something to do with the difference in their posture. Physique may also have something to do with it, but they were standing with their shoulders in an inverted triangular position and with their necks projecting straight upward from this position. One often reads in fashion magazines that the shoulders are the decisive feature that determine the look of a suit, and I could see that the line from the shoulders to the chest was taut and completely straight. On the other hand, the morning costumes that I'd seen in Japan seemed somehow rounded, with the neck and legs that protruded from the suit making the wearer look like a penguin. Such formal wear seemed to be completely unsuited to the wearer. It seemed a pity that such a costume had been created on the basis of the Western physique and posture.

Japanese and Americans differ in terms of how the neck is attached to the body. If one thinks of the torso as a socket, Japanese people feel that their neck is attached diagonally forward, in contrast to which Americans, irrespective of their ethnic origins, have a sense that their neck stretches straight up perpendicularly from the torso with the head if anything sloping slightly backward. This results in a natural balance of the centre of gravity. In other words, however much one might deliberately attempt to raise the pelvis, draw back the jaw and loosen the tension in one's shoulders in order to assume a faultless posture, it's difficult for Japanese people to maintain such a posture in the course of everyday life. We tend naturally to project our neck forward, in which case, in order to maintain the sense of gravity, we have to tilt our pelvis and naturally project the abdomen.

Looking at the portrait made during his later years of the writer Mori Ōgai, who was a member of the Meiji era elite, it is clear that Mori is projecting his neck forward. Mori studied in Europe and was an army doctor engaged in official work, meaning that he invariably appeared in public dressed in military uniform or in Western dress. But on the occasions when he wore traditional Japanese costume, it would seem that he adopted a distinctively Japanese posture. Mori continued to wear kimono in his private life and preferred to live in traditional Japanese houses. It was only natural therefore that, being immersed in such a traditional Japanese environment, he should have instantly regained a Japanese posture. But even now, more than a century on from Mori's day, we are still in a period of transition in terms of the Japanese lifestyle. There are very few Japanese people who even today enter their homes without taking their shoes off, in contrast to the almost universal custom in the West of keeping one's shoes on inside the home. When Japanese people enter their homes, they take off their shoes and begin to drag their feet along the floor. Even when there are no tatami mats in their living room, they still tend to sit on the floor rather than on chairs. In terms of the body's centre of gravity, they project their abdomen forward while their pelvis is tilted backward, with the neck stuck out in order to maintain balance. Japanese people thus adopt a posture that is clearly different from that of Westerners and we use our bodies in different ways from Westerners.

This position of the neck has an effect upon voice production. Jutting one's neck forward makes it possible to emit sounds in a slightly higher register. Japanese people tend to have relatively high-pitched natural voices. For instance, one thing I noticed in the United States when meeting third or fourth generation people of Japanese descent is how low their voices were. Although they look like ordinary Japanese in terms of facial appearance and physique, their voices sound distinctly different and they can soon be recognised on this basis alone. Their pelvis tends to be tilted slightly further back than Americans of Anglo-Saxon or African descent, but they use their bodies in daily life in a completely Western manner, meaning that their physical features such as the position of the neck are the same as those of Westerners.

Environmental considerations such as the resonance of rooms clearly had an important role to play in the development of the pure *bel canto* style of voice production used by singers in the West, and posture is an important factor in this regard. You can test this for yourself by adopting a posture in which your voice rings out resonantly and then gradually jutting your neck out forward. Your voice will get caught up in your soft palate or nose, with the consequence that the tone quality will lose its purity to obtain a rough texture similar to that employed by Japanese singers of traditional genres such *Naniwa-bushi*. The voice thus seems to be issuing from the nose or the throat, although what is actually happening is that the vocal chords in the throat are being slightly narrowed, resulting in a slight strengthening of the voice's upper register.

Tilting the pelvis also brings about changes that are evident in an analysis of vocal frequency. The voice tends to be stronger in the range of between two and four kilohertz. It gains an added sparkle in the upper register. As is clear from the computer analysis diagram, the right side is whiter.

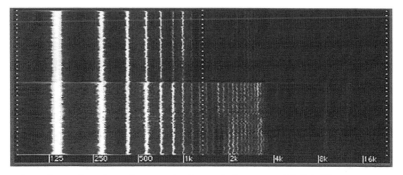

A voiceprint showing emission of the vowel 'ah'. The upper section shows the sound with the pelvis upright. In contrast, the lower section shows the sound with the pelvis tucked in.

When one adopts such a posture, the voice is affected not just in terms of pitch range but also on the level of shading and nuance. For example, a tone quality emerges with a liberal admixture of noise incorporating a guttural quality that lends itself to emotional expression in forms such as sighs and threats.

In today's Japan, a posture with the hips lowered and the neck jutting out is typified by the pose adopted by *yakuza* gangsters. Tilting the pelvis in this way no doubt benefits the yakuza in many ways. For many centuries, emphasising a stable posture that stands them in good stead when getting into a fight and emitting a voice with the capacity to scare the wits out of anyone faced by it has enabled them to demonstrate their strength to the outside world. Japanese engaged in the traditional performing arts and in traditional activities in all walks of life have preserved these physical skills. The distinctive shading and nuance that characterise such vocal production is made possible by harmonics.

What Are Harmonics?

Harmonics are elements that form part of a single sound. All sounds consist of a fundamental tone and the harmonics that accumulate above it. The fact that the same note when written on paper has a different tone depending upon the type of instrument on which it is played or the type of voice by which it is sung is due to the different harmonics that it contains. Tone and timbre are determined by the type and quantity of harmonics present in the sound. Natural sounds such as the sound of the wind or of rain, the noise emitted by cars, the speaking voices of people and the cries of animals, none of which can be represented in musical notation, all consist of a fundamental and harmonics.

Harmonics can be classified into integer harmonics and non-integer harmonics. Sounds with strong integer harmonics have a sharp, penetrating and radiant quality. A typical example of such tone colour is the *khoomii* style of overtone singing practised by the Mongols. Most Western wind and stringed instruments along with traditional Japanese instruments and traditional methods of voice production as employed in folksong are characterised by the presence in various forms of integer harmonics on a high level. Listening to such sounds may provoke initial resistance, but it has been confirmed that alpha waves are gradually emitted by the brain and it may well be because of this that people with voices with strong integer harmonics often have a charismatic quality. There are several Japanese pop singers who possess just such voices.

On the other hand, non-integer harmonics result in sounds with an impure, rough and hoarse quality, as typified especially by percussion instruments. The shakuhachi is capable of producing extremely pure, unsullied sounds, but it also has the capacity to produce breathy, wind-like sounds, as in the case of the *muraiki* technique, that include a large quantity of non-integer harmonics.

The Japanese aural sensibility appears to perceive non-integer harmonics in the same manner as language in the left side of the brain. Perhaps this is why, when Japanese people have something important to say, they unconsciously have recourse to non-integer harmonics. The acute sensitivity that Japanese possess with regard to harmonics might be ascribed to the features of the Japanese language and to living environments with little resonance.

In the West, houses and cities are generally constructed in stone. In such environments sound reverberates over and over again and gets absorbed from the upper harmonics and with the fundamental being amplified. Imagine trying to have a conversation in a swimming pool, for example. It would still be difficult to hear what the other person was saying even if subtle harmonics were to be added. In contrast, Japanese people have throughout their history lived outdoors in a humid environment amidst a plethora of plants and trees, and indoors in rooms with tatami mats and sliding partitions; that is to say in spaces with very little resonance in which harmonics rather than the fundamental are clearly perceptible. Within the sense of calm generated by Missoku breathing, the Japanese people have thus come to possess a highly sensitive awareness of tone colour and harmonics which has resulted in the extraordinary diversity and astonishing individuality, when seen in a global context, of their music.

It's interesting to observe how the extreme sensitivity that Japanese people show toward harmonics is accompanied by an unusual degree of rhythmic flexibility, in such a way that time gets distorted by harmonics. The ultimate stage in this distortion is represented by the music of the Komusō shakuhachi, in which the very notion of rhythm and meter has totally disappeared.

The Secrets of the Japanese Language

The Japanese language is a repository of harmonics. Japanese has only five vowels, far fewer than those employed in Chinese, and one of the language's main features is that sounds are invariably formed from combinations of consonants and vowels. In comparison with Korean, in which consonants can stand on their own, the number of sounds is far fewer. Conversely, all the sounds available within the language possess their own distinctive tonal quality and overtone structure. Every person brought up with Japanese as their mother tongue has continued since their early childhood to produce and recognise these sounds without the slightest hesitation.

Such accumulation of experience has enabled Japanese people to distinguish between harmonics and to produce them with their own voices and has moreover become an important element that has contributed to the formation of traditional Japanese music. But the sounds of the Japanese language in the speech of young people have changed. It has been pointed out for a long time that intonation in speech has become flat. It seems that young people have become unable to detect or to emit subtle changes in timbre.

I've already explained that abdominal breathing brings about instability in the exhalation of air, but what actually happens is that there is a crescendo in the case of exhalation and when speaking. Perfected abdominal breathing results in language with its own distinctive rhythm, but if the pelvis is erect and unstable and breathing veers between the abdomen and the chest, long phrases can no longer be supported by the breath and become abbreviated with rising intonation at the end of each phrase. Moreover, when listening to their own mother tongue, most people have almost lost the sensibility that regards such phrasing and intonation as in any way strange.

There's another interesting point to make in this regard. Many musicians who visit Japan from overseas remark negatively on the sheer volume of noise and the obtrusive music that pervades the urban environment. It's true that cities outside Japan tend to be quiet and without a constant barrage of music and announcements. Whenever I return to Japan from a visit overseas, I'm always astonished once more about incessant noise that assails people in railways stations and shops and simply when walking along the street.

I once visited a *soba* restaurant with an American saxophonist, who told me that he simply couldn't tolerate the sound of so many people slurping their noodles. It's certainly true that this involves a considerable amount of noise, although I have to say I'd never been aware of this noise myself until then. I have no idea why this is so, but Japanese people seem to have acquired the ability even in the noisiest of environments to focus their ears on a single sound within the hubbub around them.

In the book *Afōdansu to kōi* (Affordance and action), Masahiro Ōkura discusses the esoteric skills of Japanese can inspectors, known as *dakenshi*, whose job involves inspecting canned products by striking them with a short rod. By striking the can just twice, they are able to tell whether the contents are in good or in bad condition. When busy they can cope with up to five hundred cans a minute, meaning that a single dakenshi can inspect more than a hundred thousand cans in the course of a working day. Veterans in this field have outstanding ability both to produce the percussive sound and to listen to the response. Their judgment is based on their ability to distinguish between the harmonics emitted when they strike the can. What's even more astonishing is the fact that they carry out their inspections in a noisy factory environment. Apparently there isn't a single country anywhere else in the world that has incorporated this method of inspection.

It would seem that, in addition to their sensitivity to harmonics, Japanese people have acquired the sophisticated ability to distinguish between unnecessary and necessary sounds and to shut out the former.

Shakuhachi: Harmonics, Time and Space

Seen from a global perspective, the shakuhachi is a highly unusual flute which was developed in Japan to become an instrument that enables the player to control at will the quantity of integer and non-integer harmonics and thus produce a vast tonal spectrum ranging from sounds that give the impression of a sine tone with absolutely no harmonics at all to sounds suggestive of the wind that consist entirely of harmonics. The instrument might be thought of as a synthesiser developed by the Japanese long ago.

The composer, Tōru Takemitsu, described the sound of the shakuhachi as being produced vertically like a tree. What I think he was getting at is that the instrument gives rise to an extremely complex overtone structure within the context of the Zen concept of 'nothingness' (*mu*) generated by the Missoku breathing of the performer. There has been an enormous increase in the number of shakuhachi players outside Japan and especially in the United States, attracted by the unique tone quality of this instrument. Almost all these foreign players perform the music of the Komusō shakuhachi. Considering the situation in Japan, it's astonishing that these performers should wish to concentrate on the non-metrical, solo Komusō repertory in preference to the rhythmical folksong repertory and to ensemble performance with koto and shamisen.

The main reason that Komusō shakuhachi music has become a focus of worldwide interest is that it possesses a musical structure with no parallel anywhere else in the world. The main musical structures are generally determined by pitch and rhythm, but in the case of the Komusō shakuhachi these parameters are replaced by tone colour, in other words by the overtone structure, which in most musical genres plays only a subsidiary role on a structural level. Rhythm is entirely absent from this music. The musical structure of shakuhachi music is one in which harmonics exert control over time, space and the amalgam of these two elements.

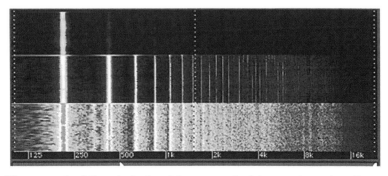

The sound of the shakuhachi as revealed in a voiceprint. From the top shows only the fundamental tone. The middle section shows the fundamental tone and integer harmonic. The bottom displays show all three layers of the fundamental tone, integer harmonic and non-integer harmonic.

Music of the Noh Theatre

The music of the Noh theatre has also undergone a highly unusual process of development whereby the priority given to harmonics has resulted in distortion that affects even scale structures. The scales of pitches employed in the music of the Noh were originally the same as those used in Gagaku court music. However, the predilection for tone colour and timbre that characterises the Japanese musical sensibility was reflected in the desire to produce harmonics. This led to the incorporation into the Noh flute of a device known as a *nodo*, which has the effect of making it impossible to play a fixed scale in tune and produces a sequence of pitches far removed from a conventional scale. In other words, the original scale of pitches that the instrument was able to produce has been distorted due to the priority given to harmonics. On the other hand, harmonics resonate in many

135

different ways within space and have a role to play in making us aware of the nature of a particular spatial environment. My own feeling is that the precedence given to harmonics in the music of the Noh theatre reflects the importance placed on the spatial aspect of this art.

Chapter 12

Missoku for People Today

The ethnologist, Tsuneichi Miyamoto, refers in one of his publications to a rural Japanese village where, when a community meeting is held, the participants do not start off by directly addressing the matters at issue. Instead, what they do is to spend hours discussing matters outside the community over a period of several days. By engaging in continuous discussions in this manner they end up not just deciding on a single matter but succeed in resolving a whole set of issues including the main matter at issue, thus putting a consensual system in place.

This is a wonderful example of an easy-going, magnanimous mode of thought; an example of rationality that embraces a wide gamut of subsidiary structures within a context wholly different from that developed in Western culture in which clear rationality is the preserve of the primary structure. This is a distinctively Japanese approach, organic and flexible, issuing from people who have built and inhabit their society.

It was more than half a century ago that Miyamoto discovered this social structure and it's doubtful whether this time consuming and laborious approach is still current in the district where he originally encountered it. Indeed, such an approach isn't likely to be feasible under conditions when it's necessary to establish communication within a short space of time with people with varying cultural backgrounds from many different countries in fields such as politics and business. However, such an approach is highly suggestive for contemporary Japanese people.

Recapturing the Spirit of Japan by Means of Missoku

The Japanese people today are going through an era of transition in many fields. At some stage Japanese people have seemed to have forgotten the technique of Missoku. The breathing they tend to practise these days tends to be shallow, but without effecting a complete transition to abdominal breathing as is prevalent in the West. Japanese people have unconsciously lost our sense of tranquillity, of stability, of concentration and of strength. The backdrop to this unsatisfactory state of affairs is formed by the sense of oppression, anxiety and lack of self-confidence that runs deep through society.

The approach to life adopted by traditional Japanese communities in the past as described by Tsuneichi Miyamoto is deeply rooted in Japanese people's bodies. Once this is realised, it becomes evident that the full richness of traditional culture ranging from daily life through to the arts is only partially accessible without recourse to the Missoku technique of breathing.

Japanese people's lifestyles have changed radically, and however much they try, they are not going to be able to turn the clock back a hundred or so years. But that doesn't necessarily mean that they can't make use of the traditional culture of breathing in modern times. It's possible to learn Missoku with a simple understanding of how our bodies work. By practising Missoku breathing we manage to awaken our innate sensual responses, thus bringing about a change in our bodies and a totally different perception of the world around us. I'd like to think that we could all retrieve this treasure and experience how wonderful it is. Giving rise to fresh potential from within our bodies and thus capturing the spirit of Japan is surely the most thrilling experience.

Bicultural Thought Processes

Being in a period of transition means that we are unable to reach the pinnacle either of our point of departure or of our destination. Missoku should not be thought of as an absolute goal. Whenever the opportunity arises it's a good idea to challenge complete mastery of abdominal breathing. Being aware of one of two options creates a knowledge of the other. In other words, by observing one option we are able to achieve two ways of seeing, feeling and thinking. We become able to accept and partake in two contrasting cultures, one with a clear primary structure and the other with a flexible, subordinate structure, in parallel, thus enabling us to expand our ways of thinking. This should inspire a sense of joy within us. If we become able at times to distinguish between the two and at other times to combine them, we will create a culture rare anywhere in the world on account of its originality. The physical memory represented by Missoku will open the path to a rich culture while giving us the key to opening up a new and bright future.

Afterword

On a visit in March 2006 to Washington DC to take part in a concert at the Kennedy Centre, I visited the Freer Gallery of Art, where I was able to see the vast collection of works by Hokusai owned by the gallery. This was the first time I'd had the chance to see so many works by Hokusai after mastering the Missoku technique.

All kinds of features that I'd never noticed before suddenly struck me with almost dizzying force. For example, a close inspection shows that all the figures depicted in Hokusai's images have tilted pelvises and bent knees; no one is depicted standing bolt upright. A totally different world opens up when one looks at these images with the image of the bent body as the standard. The closer one examines these pictures, the more one senses the links with Missoku, in terms of overall composition and of concern with detail.

The wonderful thing about this method of breathing is not just that it brings about changes in our own body but also that it changes the way in which we view the world around us. I feel certain that Japanese culture still contains vast potential that has yet to be fully explored, in forms that that are often present right next to us.

I hope that having read through this book, you may feel that something has changed within you. In order to provide as accessible as possible an entry into this field, I've tried to make the book as readable as possible. By focusing on a number of specific themes there are many related topics that I've had to leave to one side. In particular, I could have expanded in greater length on the topics of harmonics and of focusing in and out. I hope I'll have another opportunity to develop these topics in a future publication.

Akikazu Nakamura

Author Biography

Akikazu Nakamura: Shakuhachi Performer, Composer.

Akikazu Nakamura began his professional journey as a quantum chemist, having graduated from the Department of Applied Chemistry at Yokohama National University. However, it wasn't long until he turned to the shakuhachi for his future career.

Akikazu studied under numerous shakuhachi masters including Katsuya Yokohama. He then went on to study composition and jazz theory at Berklee College of Music, USA, graduating summa cum laude. He finished his tertiary studies at the New England Conservatory of Music as a scholarship student in the Master of Music Composition and the Third Stream program. His compositions are diverse and include orchestral music, choral music, chamber music, big band music, and traditional Japanese music.

He has established a performance method that makes full use of overtones, multiphonics, the traditional Japanese breathing technique of 'Missoku', and his own originally developed method of circular breathing, which involves exhaling and inhaling at the same time.

While staying true to the traditions of the Komusō monks, collecting, analysing, and performing their repertoire, he is also active as a performer of rock, jazz and classical music. He has performed in more than 150 cities in over 40 countries, at events and venues such as the Montreux Jazz Festival, Queen Elizabeth Hall (London), the Lincoln Center (New York), Blue Note (New York), the Kennedy Center (Washington DC), the Berlin Philharmonic Hall, the Polish National Opera, under the auspices of the Ministry of Foreign Affairs and the Japan Foundation. His numerous performances have been shared worldwide through over 40 broadcasting stations.

141

He has also been commissioned by NHK, the German National Radio, the Ravel Quartet in France, the Jean Sibelius String Quartet in Finland, the Munch Trio in Germany, the Saint Florent le Vieil Festival in France, the Margie Gillis Dance Company in Canada, and Music from Japan in the USA.

His CD series 'The World of Zen Music' has twice received the Japan Arts Festival Excellence Award. Additionally, he has been awarded the 19th Matsuo Performing Arts Award and the 18th Ministry of Culture Performing Arts Creation Encouragement Award for his other works. He has published 5 books in Japanese.

Akikazu has presented lectures on the structure of Japanese music, overtones and Missoku at Harvard University, Berklee College of Music, Moscow Conservatory and the University of Birmingham, Tbilisi. He has also appeared at the Kennedy Centre, the Philadelphia Composition Society, the International Centre for Japanese Studies and the University of Tokyo, among other places around the world.

He teaches at Tokyo Gakugei University, Senzoku Gakuen College of Music Graduate School, Yamanashi Gakuin University International College of Liberal Arts, Tōhō Gakuen College, and Asahi Culture Centre. He has also contributed to curriculum development of music courses in Junior High Schools at Japan's Ministry of Education.

Note to Reader

Thank you for purchasing *Breathing with Missoku*. It has been a dream of mine to finally spread my discoveries outside of Japan, and I'm thrilled that you took the time to read my book. If you would like to get in touch with questions, comments, or if you are interested in learning the shakuhachi or this breathing method online, please visit my website or social media channels:

Akikazu Nakamura website.

Akikazu Nakamura YouTube.

Office Sound Pot Instagram.

Office Sound Pot Facebook.

Office Sound Pot X.

Akikazu Nakamura Spotify.

Additionally, you can contact me at soundpot3@gmail.com.

For those who are interested in learning from me, here is an outline of the courses I provide:

- Shakuhachi: Covering repertoire from Komusō tradition to modern music.
- Breathing Classes: Missoku, circular breathing.
- Vocalisation courses: Traditional Japanese vocal techniques using overtones for theatre, recitals, singing, lecture and story-telling.
- Composition: Covering traditional Japanese music, rock, jazz, pop, classical and contemporary music.
- Improvisation: Japanese music, western classical music, jazz, and rock. Learn how to make music on the spot.

References

Akiyama, K. (1973). *Gendai ongaku o dō kiku ka* (How to listen to contemporary music). Tokyo: Shōbunsha.

Barthes, R. (1974). *Hyōchō no teikoku* (Empire of signs). Translated by Sō, S. Tokyo: Shinchōsha.

Berque, A. (1994). *Kūkan no nihon bunka* (Japanese culture of space). Translated by Makoto. M. Tokyo: Chikuma Gakugei Bunko.

Blake, W. (2022). *The Marriage of Heaven and Hell.* Argentina: Kumquat Publications.

Ishikawa, K. (2006). 'Hiragana no nazo o toku' (Solving the riddle of hiragana) in *Geijutsu Shincho,* vol. 674, (February), pp.18–82.

Kita, I. (2005). *Kokyū no shikumi* (How breathing works). Tokyo: Natsume Publishing.

Kōno, Y. (2003). *Kobujutsu ni manabu shintai sōhō* (Physical techniques to be learned from the ancient martial arts). Tokyo: Iwanami Active Shoten.

Kuki, S. (1979). *Iki no kōzō* (The structure of iki). Tokyo: Iwanami Bunko.

Lévi-Strauss, C. (2005). *Miru kiku yomu* (Look, listen, read). Translated by Nobuo, T. Tokyo: Misuzu Shobō.

Murakami, T. (2000). *Super Flat.* Tokyo: Madra Publishing.

Muraki, H. (2003). *Hakuin no tanda kokyū hō* (Hakuin's Tanda breathing method). Tokyo: Shunjūsha.

Natsume, S. (2002). *Kusamakura.* Tokyo: Iwanami Bunko.

Ōkura, M. (2001). 'Dankenshi no waza: Senrensareta kōi to afōdansu' (The technique of the can examiner: Sophisticated action and affordance) in Sasaki, M. and Mishima, H. (eds.) *Afōdansu to kōi* (Affordance and action). Tokyo: Kaneko Shobō, pp.161–195.

Saitō, T. (2003). *Kokyū nyūmon* (An introduction to breathing). Tokyo: Kadokawa Shoten.

Saitō, T. (2000). *Shintai kankaku o torimodosu* (Regaining bodily sensation). Tokyo: NHK Books.

Shinmura, I (ed.). (1976). 'Ajikan'. *Kōjien.* Second edition. Tokyo: Iwanami Shoten.

Suzuki, D. (1991). *Zen to wa nani ka* (What is Zen). Tokyo: Shunjūsha.

Takechi, T. (1969). *Dentō to danzetsu* (Tradition and rupture). Tokyo: Fujinsha.

Uchida, S. (2000). *Interia to Nihonjin* (Interior design and the Japanese). Tokyo: Shōbunsha.

Watsuji, T. (1980). *Uzumoreta Nihon* (Buried Japan). Tokyo: Shinchō Bunko.

Yatabe, H. (2004). *Isu to nihonjin no karada* (Chairs and the Japanese body). Tokyo: Shōbunsha.

Bibliography

Arai, T. (1981). *Nō to taasobi no kenkyū* (Research on agriculture and ta-asobi). Tokyo: Meijishoin.

Atsuta, Y. and Hasumi, S. (1989). *Odzuyasujirō monogatari* (The tale of Yasujirō Ozu). Tokyo: Chikuma Shobō.

Attali, J. (1995). *Ongaku, kahei, zatsuon* (Music, money, noise). Translated by Kanazuka, S. Tokyo, Misuzu Shobō.

Berque, A. (1992). *Fūdo no nihon* (Japan's climate). Translated by Shinoda, K. Tokyo: Chikuma Shobō.

Geinōshi kenkyūkai (Entertainment History Research Association). (1969). *Kagura: Kodai no kabu to matsuri* (Kagura: Ancient songs, dances and festivals). Tokyo: Heibonsha.

Griffiths, P. (2003). *Jon kēji no ongaku* (The music of John Cage). Translated by Horiuchi, H. Tokyo: Seidosha.

Habu, Y. (2005). *Ketsudanryoku* (Decisiveness). Tokyo: Kadokawa Shoten.

Haga, K. (1995). 'Nihon ni okeru iryō taijutsu ni kansuru kenkyū' (Research on Medical Taijutsu in Japan) in *Tokyo kasei gakuin daigaku kiyō (Tokyo Kasei Gakuin University Bulletin)*, 35(July), pp.393–401.

Haga, Y. (2004). *Nihonjinrashisa no kōzō* (The structure of Japanese-ness). Tokyo: Taishūkan.

Haruki, Y. and Homma, I. (1996). *Iki no shikata* (How to breathe). Tokyo: Asahi Shimbun Company.

Hasegawa, K. (2005). *Furuike ni kaeru wa tobikonda ka* (Did the frog jump into the old pond?). Tokyo: Kashinsha.

Hasumi, S., Yamane, S. and Yoshida, Y (eds). (2004). *Kokusai shinposhiumu Ozu Yasujirō tanjōbi 100 nenkinen [OZU 2003] no kiroku* (Record of the international symposium 'OZU 2003' commemorating the 100th anniversary of Yasujirō Ozu's birth). Tokyo: The Asahi Shimbun Company.

Herrigel, E. (1981). *Yumi to zen* (Zen in the art of archery). Translated by Inatomi, E. and Ueda, T. Tokyo: Fukumura.

Isozaki, A. (2003). *Kenchiku ni okeru nihon teki na mono* (Japanness in architecture). Tokyo: Shinchōsha.

Iwamiya, S. (2000). *Oto no seitaigaku* (Ecology of sound). Tokyo: Corona Publishing.

Kamata, S. (1977). *Nihon no zen goroku, dai-19 kan: Hakuin* (Japanese Zen sayings, volume 19: Hakuin). Tokyo: Kōdansha.

Karatani K. (1989). *In'yu toshite kenchiku* (Architecture as metaphor). Tokyo: Kōdansha.

Kawada, J. and Sakabe, M. (1987). *Toki o toku* (Solving time). Tokyo: Riburopōto.

Kawai, H. (1999). *Chūkū kōzō nihon no shinsō* (Hollow structure in the depths of Japan). Tokyo: Chūōkōron Shinsha.

Kazuyoshi, K. (1966). *Zen: Gendai ni ikirumono* (Zen: Living in modern times). Tokyo: Nipponhōsōshuppankyōkai.

Kojima, T. (1998a). *Uta o nakushita nihonjin* (The Japanese who lost their songs). Tokyo: Ongakunotomo.

Kojima, T. (1998b). *Ongaku kara mita nihonjin* (The Japanese in terms of music). Tokyo: NHK Library.

Kojima, T. (2005). 'Dentō ongaku ni okeru koe no denshō' (Voice transmission in traditional music) in *Dentō to bunka (Tradition and culture).* 29 (August), pp.5–9.

Kōno, Y. (2002). *Bujutsu no shin, ningen gaku* (New anthropology of martial arts). Tokyo: PHP Bunko.

Kōno, Y. (2003). *Bujutsu o kataru* (Talking about martial arts). Tokyo: Tokuma Bunko.

Konparu, K. (1980). *Nō e sasoi: Johakyū to ma no saiensu* (An invitation to Noh: The science of johakyū and ma). Kyoto: Tankōsha.

Matsuoka, S. (1994). *Kachōfūgetsu no kagaku* (The science of kachōfugetsu). Kyoto: Tankōsha.

Matsuoka, S. (2000). *Nihon suki* (Japanese suki). Tokyo: Shunjūsha.

Matsuoka, S. (2005). *Furajairu* (Fragile). Tokyo: Chikuma Gakugei Bunko.

Minami, H. (1983). *Ma no kenkyū* (Research of Ma). Tokyo: Kōdansha.

Miyamoto, T. (1984). *Wasurerareta nihonjin* (The forgotten Japanese people). Tokyo: Iwanami Shoten.

Nagae, A. (2003). *Tairana jidai* (Flat era). Tokyo: Harashobō.

Nakano, J. (1993). *Nihonjin no nakigoe* (The cry of the Japanese people). Tokyo: NTT Publishing.

Nagata, A. (2000). *Kokyū no ōgi* (The secret of breathing). Tokyo: Kōdansha Blue Backs.

Naruse, G. (1998). *Shisei no fushigi* (The mystery of posture). Tokyo: Kōdansha Blue Backs.

Nishikawa, M. (2004). *Kokutō, 1936 nen no nihon o aruku* (Cocteau, walking in Japan in 1936). Tokyo: Chūōkōron Shinsha.

Nomura, M. (1996). *Miburi to shigusa no jinrui gaku* (Anthropology of gestures). Tokyo: Chūkō Shinsho.

Ōhashi, T. (2003). *Oto to bunmei* (Sound and civilisation). Tokyo: Iwanami Shoten.

Okada, S. (1972). *Nihonjin no imēji kōzō* (Japanese image structure). Tokyo: Chūōkōron Shinsha.

Okakura, T. (1994). *Cha no hon* (The book of tea). Translated by Oketani, H. Tokyo: Kōdansha.

Panofsky, E. (2003). *Shōchō (shinboru) keishiki toshite no enkinhō* (Perspective as symbolic form). Translated by Kida, G. Tokyo: Tetsugakushobō.

Saitō, T. (2003). *Iki no nyūmongaku* (Introductory study to breathing). Yokohama: Seorishobo.

Sen, S. (1968). *Urasenke sadō no oshie* (The teaching of Urasenke tea ceremony). Tokyo: Nipponhōsōshuppankyōkai.

Sugiura, K. (1997). *Katachi tanjō* (The birth of form). Tokyo: Nipponhōsōshuppankyōkai.

Suzuki, D. (1964). *Zen to nihon bunka* (Zen and Japanese culture). Tokyo: Iwanami Shoten.

Tada, M. (1978). *Shigusa no nihon bunka* (Japanese culture of gesture). Tokyo: Kadokawa Shoten.

Takaoka, H. (1992). *Hara o nakushita nihonjin* (Japanese people who lost their hara). Tokyo: Keigado Publishing.

Takeuchi, T. (2001). *Shisōsuru karada* (The body that thinks). Tokyo: Shōbunsha.

Takeuchi, Y. (1995). *Nihonjin no kōdō bunpō* (Sociogrammar of Japanese people). Tokyo: Toyo Keizai Inc.

Takemitsu, T. (1971). *Oto, chinmoku to hakari aeru hodo ni* (Sound as strong as silence is). Tokyo: Shinchōsha.

Temman, M. (2001). *Andore Marurō no nihon* (André Malraux's Japan). Translated by Sakata, Y. Tokyo: TBS Britannica.

Tsunoda, T. (1978). *Nihonjin no nō* (The brain of the Japanese people). Tokyo: Taishūkan.

Uchida, T. (2003). *Watashi no karada wa atama ga ī* (My body is smart). Tokyo: Shinyōsha.

Uchikoshi, A. (2005). *Kokyū o kaereba genkide nagaiki* (If you change your breathing, you can stay healthy and live longer). Tokyo: Yōsensha.

Watanabe, T. (1994). *Sugata: Takehara Han, Kataoka Nizaemon* (Appearance: Han Takehara, Nizaemon Kataoka). Tokyo: Kyūryūdō.

Watanabe, T. (2001). *Utaemon: Nagori no hana* (Utaemon: The remaining flower). Tokyo: Magazine House.

Yatabe, H. (2004). *Tatazumai no bigaku* (Aesthetics of appearance). Tokyo: Chūōkōron Shinsha.

Yōrō, T. and Kōno, Y. (1993). *Kobujutsu no hakken* (The discovery of ancient martial arts). Tokyo: Kōbunsha

Photo Acknowledgements

Konishi, S. and Oka, H. (2005). *Hyaku nen mae no nihon* (Japan one hundred years ago). Tokyo: Shōgakukan.

Krafft, H. (1998). *Bonjūru Japon* (Bonjour Japan). Edited by Kazuo Gotō. Tokyo: Asahi Shimbun.

Takashina, S. (ed.). *Pikaso zenshū* (Complete works of Picasso). Vol.4. Tokyo: Kōdansha.

O-BOOKS

SPIRITUALITY

O is a symbol of the world, of oneness and unity; this eye represents knowledge and insight. We publish titles on general spirituality and living a spiritual life. We aim to inform and help you on your own journey in this life.
If you have enjoyed this book, why not tell other readers by posting a review on your preferred book site?

Recent bestsellers from O-Books are:

Heart of Tantric Sex
Diana Richardson
Revealing Eastern secrets of deep love and intimacy to Western couples.
Paperback: 978-1-90381-637-0 ebook: 978-1-84694-637-0

Crystal Prescriptions
The A-Z guide to over 1,200 symptoms and their healing crystals
Judy Hall
The first in the popular series of eight books, this handy little guide is packed as tight as a pill bottle with crystal remedies for ailments.
Paperback: 978-1-90504-740-6 ebook: 978-1-84694-629-5

Shine On

David Ditchfield and J S Jones

What if the after effects of a near-death experience were undeniable? What if a person could suddenly produce high-quality paintings of the afterlife, or if they acquired the ability to compose classical symphonies? Meet: David Ditchfield.

Paperback: 978-1-78904-365-5 ebook: 978-1-78904-366-2

The Way of Reiki

The Inner Teachings of Mikao Usui

Frans Stiene

The roadmap for deepening your understanding of the system of Reiki and rediscovering your True Self.

Paperback: 978-1-78535-665-0 ebook: 978-1-78535-744-2

You Are Not Your Thoughts

Frances Trussell

The journey to a mindful way of being, for those who want to truly know the power of mindfulness.

Paperback: 978-1-78535-816-6 ebook: 978-1-78535-817-3

The Mysteries of the Twelfth Astrological House

Fallen Angels

Carmen Turner-Schott, MSW, LISW

Everyone wants to know more about the most misunderstood house in astrology — the twelfth astrological house.

Paperback: 978-1-78099-343-0 ebook: 978-1-78099-344-7

WhatsApps from Heaven
Louise Hamlin
An account of a bereavement and the extraordinary
signs — including WhatsApps — that a retired
law lecturer received from her deceased husband.
Paperback: 978-1-78904-947-3 ebook: 978-1-78904-948-0

The Holistic Guide to Your Health
& Wellbeing Today
Oliver Rolfe
A holistic guide to improving your complete health,
both inside and out.
Paperback: 978-1-78535-392-5 ebook: 978-1-78535-393-2

Cool Sex
Diana Richardson and Wendy Doeleman
For deeply satisfying sex, the real secret is to reduce the heat,
to cool down. Discover the empowerment and fulfilment
of sex with loving mindfulness.
Paperback: 978-1-78904-351-8 ebook: 978-1-78904-352-5

Creating Real Happiness A to Z
Stephani Grace
Creating Real Happiness A to Z will help you understand
the truth that you are not your ego
(conditioned self).
Paperback: 978-1-78904-951-0 ebook: 978-1-78904-952-7

A Colourful Dose of Optimism
Jules Standish
It's time for us to look on the bright side, by boosting
our mood and lifting our spirit, both in
our interiors, as well as in our closet.
Paperback: 978-1-78904-927-5 ebook: 978-1-78904-928-2

Readers of ebooks can buy or view any of these bestsellers by
clicking on the live link in the title. Most titles are published
in paperback and as an ebook. Paperbacks are available in
traditional bookshops. Both print and ebook formats are
available online.

Find more titles and sign up to our readers' newsletter at
www.o-books.com

Follow O-Books on Facebook at **O-Books**

For video content, author interviews and more, please subscribe to our YouTube channel:

O-BOOKS Presents

Follow us on social media for book news, promotions and more:

Facebook: O-Books

Instagram: @o_books_mbs

X: @obooks

Tik Tok: @ObooksMBS

www.o-books.com

Printed in Great Britain
by Amazon

52219239R00095